MW00975704

WHY WRITE? WHY PUBLISH?

PASSION? PROFIT? BOTH? A SELF-GUIDED SEMINAR BY

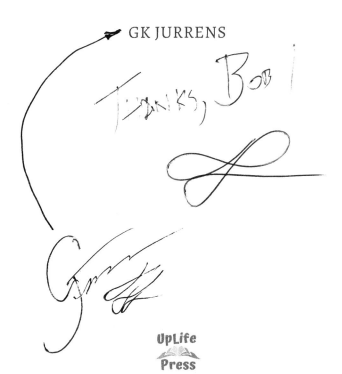

GK JURRENS

Thanks, Bob !

UpLife
Press

CONTENTS

Copyright © 2021 GK Jurrens
All rights reserved.

eBook ISBN: 978-1-952165-12-2
Paperback ISBN: 978-1-952165-13-9
v.220806_0654
GKJurrens.com

ACKNOWLEDGMENTS

~

Many thanks to the following talented authors and teachers —my favorites—for their inspiration and ideas without which we'd likely be staring at the dreaded blank page. In alphabetical order:

- Angela Ackerman / Becca Puglisi
- Charles Baxter
- James Scott Bell
- Dave Chesson
- Shawn Coyne
- Chris Fox
- Jane Friedman
- Judy Howard
- Tammy Labrecque
- David Morrell
- Derek Murphy
- Joanna Penn
- Nick Stephenson
- KM Weiland

INTRODUCTION

~

Welcome to the wide and weird and wonderful world of independent writing, editing, formatting, publishing, marketing and selling.

This *self-guided seminar* will start shallow and dive deeper as we progress. I've compiled key questions to help you crystallize your goals as a writer. I'll offer  you a tight but generous summary of information with links to incredible Internet resources that you can explore at your leisure to go deep if you wish. Take your time.

Are you struggling to find your inspiration for the book you know is inside of you somewhere? This book's initial chapters will help you get started.

Do you wonder how to efficiently start and sustain progress on this writing journey? Keep reading!

I will ask you: why should you write, and where should you start? Then what? And why should you spend your precious time and creative energy on all the *other stuff* that comprises the *business* of being an author and a publisher—you know, that which is the bane of most every author you and I know? Or should you even bother?

These simple questions usually beg potentially complex answers, but *this does not need to be complicated.* Or costly. If you don't want to do all that other stuff, don't! I *would* encourage you at least to browse through the first seven chapters of this short book, and then just write to your heart's content with a few more tools in your kit. That's okay too.

In any event, whatever your writing goals (I'll help you define them in the coming chapters), be sure to check out the comprehensive **list of resources in Appendix B.** You're sure to find useful help back there from my most treasured mentors.

If you'd like to monetize your writing talent, then into the breech, my fellow creatives! You'll appreciate countless tips from hard-won experience and research to make all that publishing and marketing stuff other than the writing itself as painless as possible, and even fun.

I will concisely unpack all of this for you. But in short, write anything you want if it pleases you. Publish if you wish, but don't make too many rookie mistakes along the way, like I did.

> **We'll drill down together on essential in-depth questions and guidance offered by dozens of experts in this brief book I call a**

viii

self-guided seminar. **Your answers should clarify your personal objectives and simplify your life as an aspiring writer, or even as an experienced** *mid-lister* **(thank you, Donald Maas).**

Steady and slow wins the race. Steady and faster wins more races.

I've focused on sharing with you as many free or cost-effective resources that have helped me on my own writing and publishing journey, and more importantly, those that accelerated my learning curve.

I offer this self-guided seminar to share with you how to make this entire end-to-end process work *for* you instead of *against* you, and hopefully, save you a great deal of time, frustration and money, especially as you first start on your own journey down this road.

For you more seasoned authors who have traveled this trail for a while, you also might snag a few ideas to pick up the pace or to enhance your profitability, or to recapture control over your precious intellectual capital.

First, who am I? My pen name is GK Jurrens. Call me Gene. I write both fiction and non-fiction. My novels include mysteries, business, political and military thrillers. Plus I write stories involving amateur sleuths and futuristic mysteries (I call them *trans-formational* mysteries). I've also recently published a poetry reader's guide and a collection of my own poetry.

But this book is my first on the craft of writing after reading and studying hundreds over the years, and after making more than a few mistakes from which I have learned out of necessity. I promise you this short resource will be different from most books on this topic you may have seen, and a great place to start your journey—*or* to pick up the pace.

 I've always enjoyed writing and playing with words. Avid blogging for the last fifteen years trained me in the writing *discipline*, first while living and traveling in our boat, and more eling in our boat, and more recently, in our motorhome. Travel inspires me, and I enjoy sharing our "on the road" experiences.

My journey as a novelist started in earnest during the winter of 2015. After attending a free writing seminar by veteran author and motivational speaker **Judy Howard** in Chandler, Arizona, Judy flipped some switch in me. After that, I went all in, stumbling and tumbling at first. I remember that wonderful feeling each time I published at least one book each year since then. So now I pay that giddy feeling forward to *you* starting with this self-guided seminar. More to come, I promise!

Twelve books comprise my *backlist* so far (including a short companion guide and three non-fiction), with another mystery series and a collection of thematic poetry chapbooks in process. Ten are currently offered worldwide in every major digital storefront. As paperbacks and eBook editions. I'm also exploring how many I wish to offer as hardcover.

Given the opportunity, I also teach paperless writing on the road. Why paperless? Well, there is limited room for a novelist's traditional tool kit such as a hardcopy library of reference books, or a *murder board,* or large *timeline charts* in an RV. No wall space! Plus, repeatedly printing hundreds of manuscript pages for editing just isn't practical, or inexpensive, or environmentally friendly—anywhere. So I use alternative approaches. I'll share with you how this is not only doable, but efficient.

I also offer in-person seminars and sell a few of my paperback editions the old-fashioned way—face-to-face, signed by the author. These are great opportunities to continue learning and sharing and networking—to stay vital and active and involved with readers. *Plus,* I make more money per paperback by selling directly to readers. This can be a non-trivial source of income. More on this later.

After six years of government service as a young man, I sold advertising, managed a hotel, was a recording engineer, studied Liberal Arts, earned a Bachelor of Science degree in Business and a Master of Science degree in Management of Technology from the University of Minnesota.

A successful three-decade career in global high-tech preceded more than a few years of sailing America's waterways, the Florida Keys, and the Eastern Caribbean—from the British Virgin Islands to near the coasts of Venezuela and Trinidad.

Until recently I enjoyed sailing, skydiving, SCUBA, sea kayaking, amateur radio, motorcycle touring, watercolor painting, creative photography and woodworking. Now I mostly write and travel with my copilot, Miss Kay with the occasional foray into *indoor* skydiving. I love crafting and playing my collection of Native American-style flutes or my treasured Japanese shakuhachi flute. So much to do!

I am the proud father of two adult children, and the equally proud grandfather of three teenage grandchildren.

My wife Kay and I now live and travel most of the time in our bus-style motorhome, having lived in forty-two states in seven years. We stop for a few weeks to a few months at a time. We find wandering North America a delightful source of endless inspiration. And let's be honest—it's fun! I occasionally share our RV adventures at **BigRigRoads. wordpress.com**.

My favorite quote? **"The difference between ordeal and adventure is attitude!"**

In addition to countless articles, blog posts and short stories, I've independently published eleven books so far (ebook and paperback editions available worldwide in all major digital store fronts, subscription and library services), including this one:

Contemporary Fiction (Thrillers):

- *Dangerous Dreams: Dream Runners: Book 1* (business/political/military drama)
- *Fractured Dreams: Dream Runners: Book 2* (political/business/military drama)

Historical Fiction (Great Depression Era Crime):

- *Black Blizzard: A Lyon County Adventure* (Rural and small-town folks clash with mobbed-up big city bootleggers)
- *Murder in Purgatory: A Lyon County Mystery* (Rural and small-town folks clash with a visiting gypsy circus)

Futuristic Fiction (Paranormal Mystery Thrillers):

- *Underground, Mayhem: Book 1* (amateur sleuthing in 2150 AD)
- *Mean Streets, Mayhem: Book 2* (second civil war quests circa 2163 AD)

- *Post Earth, Mayhem: Book 3* (humanity re-imagined in 2178 AD)
- *A Glimpse of Mayhem Trilogy: Companion Guide to the Mayhem Trilogy* (a brief survey of the chaos & symmetry of the Mayhem trilogy spanning 2150 to 2178 AD)

Non-fiction:

Why Write? Why Publish? Passion? Profit? Both? (*an eBook Seminar*—this book).

Moving a Boat and Her Crew: A Slice of Life After Retirement, Seasoned with Purpose and Adventure (nautical travelogue),

Restoring a Boat and Her Crew: Transforming an Old Yacht and Her Tenders (technical reconstruction of a fine old boat),

Poetry, Short Stories & Essays:

The Poetic Detective: Investigate Rhyme with Reason (learn to enjoy all poetry with a profound appreciation for the craft).

Coming soon: *One-Minute Stories of "Everything"* (a series of thematic chapter books featuring the poetry, original images & provocative & intensely personal essays of GK Jurrens)

Coming soon: *Running From Creeping Insanity* (a memoir of emotional survival presented as a series of short life stories)

Let's play, shall we?
Gene at GKJurrens.com
email: gjurrens@yahoo.com

OVERVIEW

WHY WRITE? WHY PUBLISH? PASSION? PROFIT? BOTH?

∾

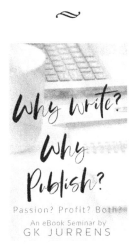

So what's with all the questions on the cover of this book? Because the genesis of this journey of discovery starts with answering a quiver of questions with brutal honesty. Here are a few more...

Have you thought of writing a book, but could use a jump-start? Maybe you just want to take your blogging to the next level? Or perhaps you're a published author looking for ideas (serious authors always are)? In any event, keep reading!

Within these pages, you can expect a grass-roots exposure to the fundamentals of six disciplines: writing, editing, formatting, publishing, marketing and selling your work, including:

The basics of authoring any writing project with a focus on the long form—like a novel, memoir or travelogue—require you to answer even more probing questions if you're serious about your writing. Most of these principles apply to both fiction and non-fiction. But don't worry. I will also provide answers from various experts to the following important questions:

- What comprises a compelling page turner, an effective plot, irresistible character and setting development?
- What needs to be on every single page you write?
- How do you effectively and methodically uncover sources of inspiration and put them to practical and efficient use?

It is also critically important that your work be candidly reviewed and critiqued by others:

- Why are critiques by other writers (and readers) so important?
- Where can you acquire useful critiques of your work for free?

What software tools best enable you to:

- Collect and optimally structure your research for a writing project?
- Organize your thoughts into useful concepts, from a first draft to a final draft?
- Efficiently format your manuscript beautifully for publication?
- Affordably publish your work to the world in both ebook and print editions?
- Provide your treasured manuscript the visibility it deserves?
- Sell what you've published?

I'll also offer you specific and practical advice compiled from dozens of my favorite industry experts specifically in the field of book marketing which includes building your own author network:

- How do you start building your own *author brand* <u>right now</u>, before you've typed, "The End?" Or even before you've started your book? And why should you?
- Where do you find sources of free, yet solid book marketing and selling advice? I will assume you are starting with no budget whatsoever. That should not stop you!
- How about a useful and extensive list of resource links to explore at your leisure?
- Or opportunities to join networks of other writers for ideas and inspiration and support?

Feel free to dwell on any or all of the following fifteen

chapters, plus **Appendix A** for a capstone case study of my current project. And check out **Appendix B** which is chocked full of outside resources because, at the end of the day, you are in charge. That's the beauty of independent publishing—control. And that's the flexibility of a self-guided seminar. *Take all the time you need. But don't wait too long to get out here on your own literary road!*

> *While we'll be focusing foremost on producing a novel (fiction), most of what I'm offering you in this book applies equally well to writing compelling non-fiction.*

So let's get started in earnest, shall we?

BRING IT ON, BLANK PAGE!

FIND YOUR INSPIRATION

THANKS TO JUDY HOWARD

∾

You'll notice I present the remainder of this book in terse non-literary bullets and lists. I call this a self-guided seminar —a series of, well, presentations. Why? Because I refuse to waste your valuable time. I only offer you concise information you need, that you can digest easily and at speed. So here we go!

A SIX-PACK TO START YOUR JOURNEY:

1. Fetch **the keys** to unlock your vision,
2. Learn how to start your **inspiration engine**,
3. Check your motivational road **map**,
4. Learn how to **rev up** your creativity engine,
5. What to do about the **potholes** and **detours**,
6. How do you check and **fuel** your creativity?

(3)

1. FETCH THE KEYS:

- Is everyone telling you, "You should write a book?"
- Do you want your children and grandchildren to know your story?
- Have you written all these journals over the years?
- Do you have all these crazy story ideas that keep you awake at night?
- If you answered any of these "yes" or "maybe," *those* are your keys!

(4)

2. HOW YOU START YOUR INSPIRATION ENGINE:

- Find the time,
- Make your writing a priority,
- Organize your workspace,

- No distractions, at least while you write,
- Make rules and find balance (between *all* of your activities),
- Exercise, socialize, take copious notes,
- Write *something*. Don't wait for inspiration,
- Join a writer's critique group,
- Use a journal of 'Writing Prompts.'

"Life begins at the end of my comfort zone." — Neale Donald Walsch

(5)

3. A MOTIVATIONAL ROAD MAP: WHAT IS YOUR GOAL?

- NaNoWriMo (annual National Novel Writing Month, a loose and fun and free competition to write your first or your tenth novel's first draft in 30 days)?
- To make people laugh?
- To inform and teach?
- To preach?
- To entertain?

(6)

4. REV UP YOUR CREATIVITY:

- What do you want to say and to whom?
- Why do you want to say it?
- What message do you want to convey?
- Have a clear intention - make a commitment,
- Have faith in yourself,
- Associate with other writers,

- Invest in your writing. Attend workshops and conferences, take seminars and peruse helpful websites. Join organizations and clubs that focus on writing and publishing. Seek local clubs. Lacking that, join online groups (more on this later). Read and study books on the craft of Writing.

(7)

5. POTENTIAL POTHOLES & EMOTIONAL DETOURS:

- What will people say?
- Who are you writing for?
- Are you any good?
- Who will care about your story?
- Do you care enough to tell your story?

- So what do you do? Move from *fear* to *trust*, especially of other writers. Clarify your goals as a writer. And then, *squeeze your eyes shut, hold your nose, and jump in!*

(8)

6. CHECK YOUR FUEL:

- You must follow your own voice —be your authentic self when you write,
- Focus on the process—do it *because* it scares you,
- Writing is healing—for the writer *and* for the reader,
- With your words, you can change the world. Or at least a piece of it.

In effect, you need to announce,

 "This is me, this is what I stand for, this is what you get when you read me. I'm doing the best I can—buy me or not—but this is who I am as a writer." —David Morrell

Take a queue from successful authors:

 "I've always had complete confidence in myself. When I was nothing, I had complete confidence. There were ten guys in my writing class at Williams College who could write better than I. They didn't have what I have, which is guts. I

5

was dedicated to writing, and nothing could stop me." —John Toland, "The Rising Sun."

" Don't quit. It's very easy to quit during the first ten years. Nobody cares whether you write or not, and it's very hard to write when nobody cares one way or the other. You can't get fired if you don't write, and most of the time you don't get rewarded if you do. But don't quit." —Andre Dubus, House of Sand and Fog

2

THE WRITING PROCESS

(9)

DO YOU WANT TO BE A WRITER? A REALLY GOOD ONE?

Are you still with me? Good for you!

At the highest level, and at the risk of stating the obvious, what's this writing craziness all about? Here is the *"dirty dozen" process* most successful  writers employ (we'll explore all this in more detail later):

1. *Capture an Idea* (which may be good or not so good, just stab the *essence* of it on the end of your quill),
2. *Write about it* (computer/keyboard, paper/pencil, parchment/quill, dictation, public restroom wall, finger-paint…),
3. *Edit* (or you'll worry forever that what you've written will never be good enough "as is"),

7

4. ***Rewrite*** (*tweak* your chicken scratchings until it's *soup*)
5. ***Repeat*** a few times (or more than a few if you're anal-retentive like most good authors) until the words that represent your idea are thoroughly marinated,
6. ***Review*** (get someone else to read and critique your fabulous manuscript, maybe a chapter at a time, both by your typical reader and by someone who is a better—more experienced, more successful—writer than you).
7. ***Publish*** (*independently*, *traditionally* or both, also known as—a.k.a.—*hybrid*),
8. ***Market/Sell*** (employ various *channels*, a.k.a. places),
9. ***Wait*** for the checks to start rolling in (don't be in a hurry),
10. ***Repeat*** (if you didn't suffer enough yet through your *Rewrite*, *Repeat* and *Review* iterations). Wear your rejections or lack of book sales like badges of courage—good things come to those who don't quit,
11. ***Move on*** (*to the next project*),
12. ***Never quit!***

3

YOUR OWN STORY COMES FIRST!

THE FIRST STORY YOU MUST WRITE IS YOUR OWN!

- *Put a pencil to your plan...* ***WRITE IT DOWN. YES, THIS MEANS YOU!***
- *Below I offer two introspective approaches to writing your own story first. I recommend using both:* (1) **The Five Ws**, *and* (2) **Twelve Goals,** many of this latter approach are answered just *yes* or *no*. Both approaches *will* clarify your objectives as a writer—without a doubt.
- *We'll then use the answers to the questions above to flesh out your brief* **Six-Point Author Business Plan**.
- *This may seem tedious, but this is an essential starting point for your personal literary journey. It worked for me, after decades of spinning my wheels. Jot down your answers to all of the questions to reveal insight into your own insanity!* ***Keep your answers and this plan.*** *A*

year from now, you'll be astounded at how far you've traveled, and whether it will be time for a new fold in your map.

With brutal honesty—that's the hardest part—document your plan by first answering the five "W" questions (do not cheat yourself—answer them all):

(10)

1. *WHO* ARE YOU WRITING FOR?

- If just for yourself, enjoy the ride. Let 'er rip!
- If for others, listen up, grasshopper. This is a lot more challenging, but a lot of fun too. This is your map!

2. *WHAT* ARE YOU THINKING OF WRITING ABOUT (BROADLY)?

- Fiction or non-fiction?
- Short stories, magazine articles? If so, which magazines? Periodicals? Historical? Fantasy? Mystery? Thriller? Crime? Romance? Adventure? Science? Topical non-fiction (cookbooks, travelogues, memoirs, instructional, autobiography, etc.)? You should read magazines before you try to write for them!

3. *WHEN* WILL YOU WRITE?

- Occasionally? Every day?

- When will you start? If not today, why not?

4. *WHERE* WILL YOU WRITE?

- At home? Outdoors? Coffee shop? Why not *anywhere*?

5. *WHY* DO YOU WANT TO WRITE?

- This is tough to answer, but it's important to think about this stuff to set appropriate goals as you embark on your literary trip.
- The only wrong answer? *You just like the **idea** of being an author!*

HERE'S HOW *I* ANSWERED FIVE "W'S" (FOR MYSELF):

1. *FOR WHOM* AM I WRITING?

- Mostly for myself, but I'd like to be taken seriously as a writer by others as well,
- I want to be a *good* writer and a published author,
- Decent sales and five-star reviews are nice too, but not essential for my emotional well-being.

2. *WHAT* DO I WANT TO WRITE?

- I've written a lot of non-fiction. I also write fiction and poetry. Mysteries seem to be my sweet spot right now; although I also enjoy writing a non-fiction book like this one. I favor the mystery genre in fiction, but I am also exploring thrillers, drama, including my recent interest in historical crime fiction.

- My characters and venues (locations or settings) are based on my personal life experiences. I feel I have a lot to say about that (I've been blessed with an interesting life).

3. WHEN WILL I MAKE TIME TO WRITE?

- Initially, I found time to write here and there, and often no more than fifteen to thirty minutes at a time.
- Now I'm committed to writing *something* every day for an hour or more (sometimes much more). That might be a blog post, researching, drafting or editing a scene in one of my current works in progress, writing or responding to emails related to writing, social media posts associated with writing, compiling or refining new book ideas, or working on a non-fiction book like this one. I even take notes on my phone at the grocery store, maybe I jot down an interesting phrase, a cool rhyme, or text the wife to see if we need almond milk.
- My target is writing or editing at least a thousand words per day (just 4 pages of prose). I almost always exceed that. When I don't, I make up for it *mañana.*
- I'm convinced that consistent practice is key to improving my skills as a writer (or *any* skill).

4. *WHERE* WILL I WRITE?

- I write mostly on my laptop computer in the motorhome (where my wife and I live most of the time), or on my iPad (with a BlueTooth keyboard) *anywhere*. I once carried a small paper notebook to jot down interesting details about people, places or things. Lately, that's my smartphone's note-taking app. I can't afford to lose juicy details I observe around me all of the time—anywhere—or moments of inspiration that I need to capture ASAP (my memory isn't what it used to be).
- I take notes standing in the grocery cashier line awaiting check-out. I've made character notes observing people at the doctor's office (even odors!). Airports and campgrounds are also fertile ground. Again, *anywhere and everywhere!*
- My best writing springs from observing the *details* in my own life and *imagining further* with those details as starting points.

5. *WHY* DO I WRITE?

- I love writing. I think about writing a lot. I cannot imagine not writing.
- I can toy with a single digital photograph for hours to make it just right. I enjoy doing the same with words and a story. **KM Weiland** calls sickos like us *word players.* I like that. Thanks, Katie.
- I chose to write a short **600-word article that describes why I write.** That helped clarify my thinking. It might help you too. This article also illustrates my author's *voice* (more on that later).

Holler if you need help accessing this article. I'm at gjurrens@yahoo.com.

(11)

MORE SPECIFICALLY

These five "W"s beg twelve more specific *goal-oriented questions.* Any answer for each is fine—as long as it is honest and right for *YOU*:

1. Do you simply wish to improve your personal journaling?
2. Will you create and maintain a blog for personal use? For professional use?
3. Do you wish to write a better, more compelling short story? A novella (short novel)? A chapbook (chapter book) of poetry?
4. Is it easy for you to write, or is it a struggle?
5. Do you like to spend time playing around with words you've written to get them to perform for you in just the right way?
6. Do you love to learn how to do things better over time?
7. Does it matter how many books you sell? Or whether you sell any? Or is finishing one book all you care about? Maybe you only offer them as unique gifts—a window into your soul?
8. Do you have a day job (including retirement) or are you planning to be a full-time author (definitely *not* retirement)?

9. Are you willing and able to dedicate time each and every day to improving your craft, in addition to actually spending time writing?
10. If you intend selling your book(s), will you do your own marketing and do you have the desire (and discipline) to do so?
11. If you do but don't already have the skills and experience, are you willing to learn how to market your own work? If not, can you afford to pay someone else in time or money (editors, agents, publishers, ads)?
12. Are you willing to build your own *fan base,* to build your *platform*, your *brand*?

If you can be ruthlessly honest with these starter questions, you will gain a clear sense of how far down the rabbit hole you'll want to shimmy. *However far you wish to go, this book will help you attain your goals, or to find the help to do so.*

Nobody answers <u>all</u> these questions *the same*. But you do need to understand if your love of writing is compelling enough that you're willing to devote time, energy and a large piece of your soul to this work. Or is this just a casual interest? A hobby? If so, *that's okay too.* These questions are just intended to position yourself in the writing realm! They also help you talk with other writers in a meaningful, honest *and specific* manner. Answers to these invasive questions also provide you a useful reality check to help you best plan your writing journey.

Did you answer all twelve questions *and* write down your answers? If so, good job. If not, go back and do so. You'll use these answers in the final stage of documenting your career plan as an author, even if it's just for one article, one short story, or one novel.

> "Every good book, every bad book, and all the great books, too, were written a little at a time. A day's work, over and over for a period of months or years" —*Richard Bausch*

> "A true novelist is one who doesn't quit." —*John Gardner*

> "The best way to predict your future is to create it." —*Abraham Lincoln*

YOUR BASIC AUTHOR BUSINESS PLAN:

Now it's time to pull it all together. This may seem tedious, but it's important to finish *your* story before you write others. Let's articulate **six planning objectives**. See my answers below, circa 2016, approximately one year after I decided to seriously attack the craft of writing. Keep your own answers above close at hand to help you document your objectives below. Then we'll conclude this chapter and *methodically* approach the topic of writing:

1. **Vision**: I wanted to write at least one novel, maybe more. I knew this would be a huge undertaking. *My novel* (sounds nice, doesn't it?) would take thousands of hours and a year or more to complete. I was okay with that. After I almost immediately decided that I had more than one book in me, I wanted the second book to be easier, so I studied lots of books on how to write well and efficiently in order to accelerate my learning curve.

2. **_Strategy_**: I wished to sell some books, mostly to understand that part of the business, but I didn't need to make a living from them. If the money happened, terrific. I'd buy a new RV from book profits. This was a fantasy, but I recognized it for what it was. I still depended on my savings and my pension. After all, I wasn't a complete idiot—yet. That could change!

3. **_Investment_**: I was willing to spend a few thousand hours spanning six to eighteen months not only writing, editing and accepting, even seeking brutally honest critiques of my debut work from other writers, but also re-writing, learning as much as I could about the craft of writing, and talking with other writers about writing. Maybe a few editors and agents and publishers too. Maybe not. I didn't have a lot of money to spend or patience to wait years for a book to get published, so I chose to use as many free or cheap do-it-yourself resources as possible to independently (self) publish. At least initially. Traditional publishing might or might not come later. After all, I was approaching seventy-one years of age and I still wanted to do other stuff. Lately, I've chosen to invest not only time, but some money (for productivity). *But I decided I would never pay anyone else to publish my work. That's not how it's supposed to work!*

4. **_Networking_**: I *love* being with other people who share my passion, whatever that may be at any moment in time: RVs, sailing, skydiving, kayaking, amateur radio, woodworking, performing music, watercolor painting and of course, writing! So I

made a point of being with these sorts of folks
every chance I got.

5. *Pressure*: I wanted no deadlines, other than those I
imposed upon myself. If I subjected myself to such
pressures, I might not enjoy writing as much. So I
avoided the risk of accepting big monetary
advances with commensurate project schedules or
high-pressure freelance gigs. Now if I could just
get that six-figure advance without all that other
stuff….

6. *Balance*: I was not flying solo. That meant I needed
my *much better half* to tolerate my passions. She's
been sort of okay with these objectives. *But* she
only knows about *some* of the time I spend writing.
The rest of the time I sneak it in while she's
sleeping (she knows, and I pretend she doesn't
know, but I know she knows). I also remain patient
with *her* passions. It's all about balance.

After baring my soul to write this stuff down, I had a
good idea where I really stood. Writing is fulfilling, *but challenging if you want to do it well.* You can't go wrong by *really*
knowing where you stand. Said another way, *how do you
know where to go if you don't know where you are?*

    "Apply your heart to discipline and your ears to
words of knowledge." —*Proverbs 21:12*

    "There is no knowledge won without sacrifice."
—*The Buddha*

Now set your answers and this plan aside for periodic
review, perhaps in your *author journal,* and let's move on.

Pro Tip: *By now, you should know that if you meet serious authors (and you should seek them out), you should be getting the idea that theirs is damn hard work. They do **not** want to hear you say, "Yeah, I've thought about writing a book," as if it's a trivial pursuit that you just haven't gotten around to yet. But asking them for advice once you've decided to write? That is very cool.*

4

THE BASICS OF WRITING YOUR NOVEL

~

When you're first embarking on your literary journey, use some of the lists in this book as *checklists* to stay out of the ditch on story structure, how to craft compelling villains and heroes, settings, plots, twists, etc. Then drill down into expert resources to continue building your skills efficiently and with efficacy. Don't worry—soon, all of this will become second nature to you. But you *gotta wanna.*

Even if you're an experienced author, you will still pick up new ideas or maybe snag reminders of those you'd forgotten. Anyone can write, but not everyone is willing *and* able to consistently do what it takes to write well.

As an example, if you like to ski, do you want to glide down the tame bunny hill with serenity, or fly down the killer slopes screaming with delight? Are you okay hanging out with the bunnies, or are you a bad boy or girl with a burning desire to take some chances? Either way is okay, but your eyes should be wide open *before* hitting the wrong slope.

You'll find it's the same with writing. If you have some natural writing skills, that's great. Your desire to write well— to grab and hold a readers' attention—will then largely be driven by your ability to sustain your enthusiasm while learning to improve your writing, *and by practicing it regularly.* If you feel you really don't possess a lot of natural talent, so what? Study the craft, practice and get it done!

Just like skiing. Or poker. Or sex. I'll provide some ideas, motivation and resources (not the sex part).

You must provide the action. Unless you choose to remain a spectator. Then doing little or nothing here is okay too. But don't fool yourself. You're better than that. Like anything, *writing is ten percent inspiration and ninety percent perspiration.* After all, you *are* reading this book. I'm going to help you spot your brilliance and sweat—a little or a lot is up to you. So let's continue our journey.

(12)

SIX ESSENTIAL ELEMENTS FOR EVERY MODERN AUTHOR:

1. **Time** (to think, research, observe, write…)

2. **Discipline** (to write, read, edit, read *aloud*, edit again, join critique groups who offer embarrassingly honest and constructive criticism, read again, edit again….),
3. **Computer** (for researching, writing, storing, archiving…),
4. **Internet** access (for research),
5. **Author Software** (for writing, organizing, formatting),
6. **Smartphone, tablet, paper notebook/pen** (for field notes, reading, reaching out to sources).

*[**Personal note:** I believe one of my own most curious and perhaps valuable traits as a writer is the enjoyment I derive from reading my own work, but through my ideal readers' eyes and from within my own ego's vulnerable armor.]*

(13)

A TRIO TO GET STARTED:

1. *Book Idea:* Jot down a draft premise (initial summary of your entire book) in a few paragraphs. Refine it over a period of days or weeks until it *exactly* reflects the book you wish to write (more on this later). Start with "what if" questions, what's expected/unexpected from the answer for each question; Review all of that; Then write a refined two-sentence premise. Then jot down the book's *logline* (a screenwriting term)*:* such as, "***A*** (descriptor) (protagonist) ***must*** (do something) ***that will*** (set up) ***a*** (climactic encounter) ***with a*** (descriptor) (antagonist)." As an example, the *logline*

for my book, *Mayhem: Underground*: **"A mind-reading ex-priest must protect the love of his life which will not only ex-communicate him from his beloved Church, but may very well get him killed in a clash with a nefarious government assassin."**

2. *Outline or not*: Are you a *plotter* (a planner) or a *pantser* (write by the seat of your pants)? Either way is okay, but be mindful of overall story structure no matter what (more on all of this later). For example, I start with information that expands on the book idea (*logline*) above with a list of *big moments* in the storyline, each with its own juicy complicating factor, and how that will make your protagonist more interesting but also more uncomfortable. I list what additional settings (locations) each complication will require. I do this for each major and minor character (protagonists, antagonists, sidekicks, love interests…), identifying which has the most potential for drama. What are motives for each? Goals? Values? How will antagonists attack the protagonist's weaknesses in different ways? Then I create a scene list and connect the dots (later, see the use of *Outlining Your Novel Software* for more insights in Chapter 6) which will help you to more easily keep track of all these details which are so important in creating a compelling story that readers will fall in love with.

3. *First Draft*: Once you start the actual writing process, capture the entire first blush of your manuscript, beginning to end, without editing. Just write. Please! ***Pro tip:*** *A crappy but complete first draft is precisely your objective.*

(14)

WHEN YOU GET STUCK IN THE MUCK:

1. Be of good cheer (getting stuck in the quagmire on the writer's road is an inevitable encounter - embrace the experience, learn from it, review this book or others on the craft of writing),

2. Re-organize (if you get lost in all of your detailed research. Regroup, list your details a different way, e.g., by character, by scene, by setting...),

3. Writing prompts (Internet search for *writing prompts* to get you out of the mud),

4. Observe life happening all around you, in detail. How can you use it to add depth and spice to your writing?

5. Read a good book within your genre. Pay attention. Does it make sense? Does it flow? How does it relate to your current project?

6. Take a break (physical exercise, physical work, what occurs to you? Take and review fresh notes),

7. See a good movie (watch it like a writer).

(15)

TARGET-RICH ENVIRONMENTS FOR YOUR WRITING:

- Write blog posts, magazine articles, memoirs, short stories, novellas, novels, poetry, screenplays… Identify your passion and feed it!

(16)

WHAT MAKES A GOOD STORY?

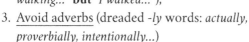

1. Show, don't tell (convey action/movement, minimize descriptive narrative),
2. Use active verbs (**not**, *"I was walking…"* **but** *"I walked…"*),
3. Avoid adverbs (dreaded *-ly* words: *actually, proverbially, intentionally…*)
4. Avoid abstract words (*pretty, ugly, love, hate…*),
5. Use the senses (actions, dress, habits, what did s/he ***do***?). **Not** *"the house smelled good."* **Instead**, *"the scent of pine needles tingled his nostrils as he entered the house."*

(17)

BUILDING CHARACTER:

1. All books are about characters (usually people, sometimes animals or lively inanimate objects),

2. *Not* about *what* happened,
3. *Is* about people who need a
   miracle… victims, criminals,
   what people *do* when something
   happens,

4. *Characters* <u>are</u> what they say, to whom they say it
   and how they say it,
5. *Dialogue* builds characters.

(18)

PLOT AND STRUCTURE:

1. Engaging *conflict* builds to
   a crescendo,
2. The *protagonist* must
   attempt to overcome
   conflict,

3. The *antagonist* causes conflict, but protagonist does
   too, or reacts to it,
4. First attempt to overcome usually makes things
   worse.

(19)

PLOTTING A COMPELLING STORYLINE:

1. Plot should be composed of *a
   series of conflicts* within and
   between characters—also called
   tension: internal <u>and</u> external
   conflict that is *personal*,

2. *Protagonist* must fail many times before succeeding,
3. Protagonist's story is only as interesting as the *antagonist* makes it – the more daunting, the better,
4. Remember... ***punish your characters!*** Your readers will love you for it.

(20)

Your book's *opening scene* is critical. You should nail the following elements **in every scene** but **especially** in the first scene of the first chapter to <u>hook</u> the reader into continuing to read:

1. <u>Conflict</u>,
2. <u>Action</u>,
3. <u>Suspense</u>,
4. Make it <u>plausible</u>,

5. <u>Active verbs</u> ("they expected us," *not* "we were expected"),
6. <u>Be specific</u> - no abstract words (instead of "pretty" or "ugly", use actions, dress, habits...),
7. <u>Use the senses</u> (describe smells, sounds, weather, texture of the setting and how a character responds it),
8. <u>Who are your characters</u> (describe *actions* that tell you what kind of people they are),
9. <u>Dialogue</u> (what they talk about, or don't talk about, slang, expressions unique to certain characters...),
10. <u>S.U.E.S.</u> **S**omething **U**nexpected in **E**very **S**cene! — thanks, James Scott Bell.

A CASE STUDY:

Let's dissect the *opening scene* of my recent novel, **Mayhem: Mean Streets**. You'll read the scene's text in **bold**, I'll offer commentary within brackets *[...] in light italicized text*. Note that while this scene comes to you from a specific genre (a dystopian paranormal mystery), the same principles apply more broadly to any story—fiction *or* non-fiction.

Later in this book, we'll explore all underlined aspects noted below after we examine the text of the following scene.

This case study will reveal some literary devices (techniques that are underlined below), some of which we have not yet explored, but don't worry. We'll cover them all in subsequent chapters. Trust me, and just have some fun! Here we go...

Final cover art for "Mayhem: Mean Streets," the second book in a futuristic mystery/thriller trilogy by GK Jurrens. As we must edit our writing, this cover is the final version of a dozen or more variations before I settled on this one. A good cover will identify the genre with the title, color theme, appropriate graphics, and most importantly, inspire a shopper to read the book's description on its back cover or online sales page.

A BATTLE

[An evocative chapter title alludes to action & conflict. "A" Battle suggests there will be more than one.]

The Digs
[A setting that immediately raises a question in the reader's mind... "The Digs?" What? This will keep them reading]
Under Old Chicago,
[More questions arise. Under? Old? But a familiar city to ground the scene in a familiar geographical reality. Sort of...]
Williana
[What?!]
United Westican Territories (UWT)
[Okaaay, where?]
August 2163
[When: sets the story on a specific future timeline; sets the reader's expectation]

*[So with a carefully chosen chapter title and by establishing the setting on a specific timeline, we've already planted a **bunch** of questions in the reader's mind without asking a single question (subtext). I hope I've hooked the reader into an insatiable desire to continue reading, at least for the next page or two. We're dangling the hook by appealing to their sense of curiosity]*

Always the same, always different. Solitude helped, if he could find it. But solitude proved illusory.

[Unasked and unanswered questions. We're further setting the hook (drawing the reader in) by immediately engaging the reader's imagination and interest; active verbs: helped, proved; contrast: always vs illusory; builds reader's curiosity; theme: solitude mentioned twice in a single short paragraph.]

Molten knives stabbed Birdman's eyes, teased of abating, but did not.

[More hook: what's going on here? Keep reading to find out; senses engaged: molten = heat; strong verb: stabbed; active verb: teased; compelling character: unusual name (Birdman); oh, and so a main character is introduced in the second line of the book) who gets his eyes stabbed? But why? Keep reading to find out!]

Closed-mouth screams layered onto whispered shouts of muttered desperation, of professed love, of certain death.

[Suspense: something's happening already, only five sentences in, but we're still not sure what; conflict: layered, opposing emotions; of the senses: sound (screams); surprising contrast: closed-mouth screams with whispered shouts? Love and death both mentioned in the same sentence? And this is just the end of the first paragraph. Keep reading...]

Yes, it all came to him, even the deep-exhale surrenders of those who were crossing the final dark line of that profound transitory event itself.

[Hints at a satisfying resolution of some sort: ...it all came to him...; More suspense and building toward a little mystery: references enigmatic events. Yup, keep reading!]

Ironically, those dark crossings clawed at his pain centers the least, as they, unlike the others, offered a lightness, a final unbounded freedom. But all the others...

*[Building tension (dark crossings) **and** easing inner conflict at the same time with some closure: lightness, final, freedom; are we talking about the freedom of dying here? Already?; strong verb:*

WHY WRITE? WHY PUBLISH?

clawed; More questions than answers: But all the others... What others?]

"She loves me... That's a lie... She knows... The best day of my life?... Cinnamon, sage, boiled cabbage... I HATE YOU!... So wonderful... My eyes—can't breathe!... Please don't die!... I'll do anything... Shots fired/officer down/how many?/aghhhh..."

[Shows (doesn't tell) through the senses via Birdman's internal monologue: cinnamon, sage, boiled cabbage all suggest odors; sight: eyes; sound: shots fired; conflicting and seemingly random and overwhelming emotions that build suspense; continues the hook: what the hell is going on here? You know it, keep reading...]

"Sir? You okay? Sir?"

[Initial dialogue introduced early; in a youthful vernacular which creates this character's voice and establishes a relationship of respect: Sir?]

Birdman's intense yellow eyes looked like they would burn a hole through the glass of the only window in his small apartment. The boy followed his mentor's intense gaze, only seeing the flame of a huge candle resting on a small table near the cracked and peeling window sill.

[Paints a picture in the reader's mind of a compelling character: intense yellow eyes; setting: small apartment, only window, huge candle; senses: sight: flame; specificity: only window, cracked and peeling window sill]

And suddenly, those deep-set dark eyes twinkled with warmth and immediacy once again. Like before.

[Contrast and conflict: inner conflict from within this compelling character: dark eyes twinkled; contrast: distant intensity vs warmth & immediacy; specificity: deep-set (eyes)]

"Sorry? Oh, now where and when were we? Ah, yes. Be patient. You must remain positive and hopeful, even during dark times. This moment is *your* moment, no one else's. Now finish your tea and go ask her, like we rehearsed. All right, m'boy?"

*[Expand on the plausible character's demeanor: absent-minded, encouraging, incites action, an early plant to set up a theme in the story: displaced in time (where **and when** are we?), and alludes to dark times; further defines the scene with specific actions and movement (drinking tea, go ask) and refers to an offstage character (her)]*

He smiled at the shiny young man, punishing the few soft chin hairs on which he unconsciously tugged. There were so few young ones.

*[Continues the hook: **why** so few young ones; plausible: young man with soft chin hairs and unconscious habits; strong verbs: tugged, punishing, further develops a picture in the reader's mind of the young man with an unusual adjective (shiny) which suggests subtextual attributes]*

Birdman also smiled at the wonder of the human spirit and of adolescent infatuation. But most of all, he smiled because he so needed to cherish this treasured moment, unsure of how many more in which he would be privileged to indulge.

[Compelling character: Birdman's emotion, wonder and empathy,

need for treasured moments of simple pleasure, adolescent infatua-
tion; Suspense: tension... uncertainty over the future?]

"Um, thank you, sir. You're the best."

[Dialogue in voice]

"No, thank *you*, m'boy, for reminding me how precious
every breath of life should be, every thought, every
emotion. Now forget the tea you're just pretending to
enjoy. Go find her and ask her. Right this moment. Go!"

[Something unexpected: find her and ask her? What?; action: Go!
Further develops Birdman's patriarchal character]

After a brief homage to his mentor, the boy sprang for the
door before he had thoroughly untangled his spindly legs.
He tripped on the frayed edge of the ragged old rug upon
which they sat. The partially filled teacup at his feet
upended with a tinkle and a splash.

[Resolution: you can sense this initial scene is winding down:
After...; action verbs & movement: sprang, untangled, hoisted,
upended; senses: tinkle, splash; specific: partially filled; texture &
specific: frayed, ragged; unexpected: teacup upended]

He stumbled, cast an embarrassing glance over his
shoulder at the wide-grinning Birdman and mumbled,
"sorry..." as he grabbed the ancient brass knob.

[Action verbs: stumbled, cast, mumbled, grabbed; specific: wide-
grinning, ancient brass knob; Dialogue: "sorry..." with much left to
be imagined as subtext]

The warped portal stuck and creaked as the boy jerked it open against some protest. It was actual wood, a rare commodity possessed of endearing quirks. Wood seemed happiest when being worked. That door remained closed more than not.

[Senses: creaked; action verbs: stuck, creaked, jerked; Subtext: Wood is rare in the future, door remained closed more than not]

Birdman bathed himself in a warm glow as he heard the boy clomp down the narrow stairs, also wooden, also creaking with delight. A puppy whose feet were too big, he would be a tall one.

[Compelling characters and setting: bathed in a warm glow, boy clomping; metaphor: compared to a growing puppy, a tall one]

Puppies. A distant memory... from before.

[Plausible memory: puppies; unexpected: no more puppies? Why? Why a distant memory? Before what event? Before? Before what?]

And then it began anew, but with less scat...

[Transition: the story continues; choice of unusual word: scat (feces found in the wild on a trail) as a metaphor; Yet another hook question: what began anew? Ah, the internal monologue, of course.]

"What would Birdman say?... I love this place... will I ever be with child?... need a trip to the lower tunnels to fetch water... will you trade a head of cabbage for two carrots?..."

[Reveals a sense of place or setting: lower tunnels, trade, agrarian culture. Attracts the reader into further engagement with the

settings and more <u>normal character activities</u> (possible pregnancy, fetching water) and <u>interactions</u> (bartering for basics)] •

Assuming you like the genre, does this two-page opening scene <u>hook</u> you, and compel you to keep reading? If so, why? If not, why not? What would you change? Perform the same analysis of your own opening scene, but only after you've completed the entire first draft of your story (please puke out the whole manuscript before you start "polishing," but ultimately, you *will* polish your scenes—ad nauseam). And don't worry about underlined terms above that we haven't yet discussed. We'll get to them all.

Pro tip: *Never fear shuffling scenes around to maximize dramatic effect once you step back and look at your completed manuscript. For example, I moved the scene we just dissected to the second scene in the published version of* **Mayhem: Mean Streets***; however, I held the new opening scene to these same high standards. Feel free to preview ("look inside") Mean Streets by GK Jurrens on your favorite digital store front's sales page.*

Let's move on and drill down...

(21)

PLOT:

1. The <u>plot</u> of a story is composed of the writer's choice of <u>events</u> in order to tell the story of the character's progression toward a <u>goal</u> or <u>desire</u>

35

while overcoming <u>obstacles</u> usually caused by the villain's (<u>antagonist's</u>) <u>actions</u>,

2. <u>Trust your reader</u> to figure some of it out (don't spoon-feed your reader),
3. <u>Show</u> (through actions), <u>don't tell</u> (with long boring narratives and descriptions).

SPECIFIC CHARACTERS:

(22)

The <u>antagonist (villain)</u> must always have the advantage:

1. They must test the hero's <u>values</u> and <u>morals</u>,
2. Should be aware of the hero's <u>flaws</u>,
3. Must not be entirely evil. For example, your villain(s) must seem normal, likable, possibly even endearing,
4. The reader *must* have an understanding of *why* he/she is evil.

(23)

The <u>protagonist (hero)</u> must be relatable:

1. Must have a <u>goal</u>,
2. Must <u>risk</u> something,

3. Must have <u>flaws</u> that prevent him from solving the tragedy,
4. The reader must think, "This could happen to me. What would *I* do?"
5. <u>Conflict</u> must develop gradually and credibly,
6. Begin with a sense of unease,
7. "Show me a hero, and I'll write you a tragedy." —F. Scott Fitzgerald.

(24)

Possible supporting characters:

- <u>Love interest</u>
- Best <u>friend</u> (supporter, optimist, skeptic)
- Comedian or <u>jokester</u>
- <u>Teacher</u> (in a literal sense)
- <u>Mentor</u> (wise role model)
- <u>Boss</u>
- <u>Parents</u>
- <u>Siblings</u>
- Nosy <u>neighbor</u>

- Nemesis
- Cute sidekick
- Antagonist's henchmen
- Traitor

(25)

Results of conflict:

1. Protagonist must attempt to overcome the conflict(s),
2. Usually the first attempt makes things worse,
3. Protagonist makes more serious mistakes because of his stress,
4. Does each twist of the plot force the protagonist to deal with his inner issues, his flaws?
5. Each attempt alters or improves the character,
6. Each significant event has to be more significant than the last.

Building character:

1. Who is your character?
2. Show your character in a classic (character-revealing) moment: Waking up in the morning, waiting in a long line,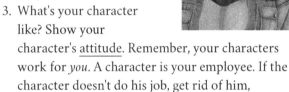
3. What's your character like? Show your character's attitude. Remember, your characters work for *you*. A character is your employee. If the character doesn't do his job, get rid of him,
4. Make your characters vulnerable. Make them stop and think. Give them strong opinions,
5. Make one character sacrifice or risk something for another,
6. Combine characters if you have too many (for example, a drunken cousin and a courageous friend simplify to a drunken but courageous cousin).

Major Characteristics:

1. A character must exhibit the characteristics of her job,
2. Let them explore beyond their jobs,
3. Use all of your characters! But don't use too many!

4. Make them <u>vulnerable</u>: a disability, suffered injustice, sacrifice, misplaced loyalty, hopelessly in love with the wrong person...

<u>Interview</u> each of your characters before beginning to write:

- See ideas for character construction on **K.M. Weiland's site,** *Helping Writers Become Authors,*
- Lots of other good (free) stuff on this site too!

For example, get to know each of your characters in detail *before* you begin to write, which will further fuel your inspiration engine. Here is a handy checklist. Use your interview results for each character as you write about them:

- <u>Reference photo</u>: use an image (photo) to inspire you, to spark your feelings for this character,
- <u>Name</u>: for fiction, consider using a name generator, e.g., within Scrivener—Edit/Writing Tools/Name Generator—or an online name generator,
- <u>Role</u>: major or minor protagonist, antagonist, other (see list of possible character roles discussed above),

- Background: address, phone number, jobs, salary, travel, friends, enemies, how others view them, who they live with, fight with, spend time with, who they *wish* to spend time with, who depends on them, people each most admires, enemies, dates, marries. Do they have children?
- Outlook: optimistic, pessimistic, real, feigned, does he like himself, what would he change about himself, personal demons, is he lying to himself about something, morality level, confidence level, a typical day, words he'd use to describe himself, how others describe him, greatest joy, greatest pain, things everyone knows about him, things no one knows that will develop with the story,
- Appearance: physical build, posture, head shape, eyes, nose, mouth, hair, skin, tattoos/piercings/scars, voice, clothing, what people notice first, mouth, clothing, how would she describe herself, how would others describe him, his health, disabilities, handicaps,
- Characteristics: her love language, how much self-control does she possess? What are her fears? What makes her angry or cry ? Strongest and weakest character traits, talents, what people like best about her,
- Interests: religious or political leaning (tread carefully and deliberately - this can easily alienate readers), collections, food, music, books, movies, sports/recreation, did he play in school, ethnicity, best way to spend a weekend, a great gift for him, pets, vehicles, large possessions and his favorites,
- Attitude: when is he happy, angry, frustrated, sad, afraid, idiosyncrasies, laughs/jeers at, ways to cheer him up, ways to annoy, hopes, dreams, and

how does he see himself accomplishing them? Worst thing he's ever done to someone and why, greatest success, biggest trauma, biggest embarrassment, what he cares most about in the world, his secrets? If he could do one thing and succeed, what would it be? What do you love most about this character, why will readers sympathize,

- Demeanor: how will his voice sound on the page, how is this person ordinary or extraordinary? Describe an interesting anecdote (a defining moment)—is this situation ordinary/extraordinary? What is this character's core need? His history?

Even though you might not plan to use all of this in your story for each major character (you probably won't), you might be surprised and wish to leverage more than you initially imagined to create undeniable authenticity in your characters, maybe even in surprising ways. It's all important stuff to explore before you start writing, when you get stumped, or when your characters seem flat or two-dimensional. Flesh them out! Know them better than your reader!

(28)

BUILDING A STORY:

1. A story is about people (your reader must care about them),
2. People = *characters,*
3. Story is about what people *do,*
4. Action = *plot,*
5. *A good story = a good plot,*

6. A *good plot* = descriptive *scenes*, believable *characters*, *action* and *suspense*.

So what makes a *great* story?

First, you need an opening scene that hooks the reader (but you already know that) and then continue in every single chapter to keep the reader involved and wanting more with every page:

1. Conflict with action and suspense,
2. Imagery that profoundly draws the reader into each scene,
3. Characters that the reader cares about in a profound way.

Second, you offer a plot that keeps the reader engaged with:

1. Continued action and suspense,
2. Your plot moves along at an engaging clip (*it cannot drag*)!
3. Sprinkled-in descriptions that keep the reader lost in the complexity of the characters' dilemmas (but *no massive info dumps*, please),
4. Your reader is always trying to imagine, "What would *I* do if I were that character?"
5. Readers root for your characters who struggle and should be struggling in every chapter.

A conclusion that *compels* the reader to:

1. Feel good that he has stood by the characters like a good friend throughout their experiences of conflict,
2. Be *enlightened* in some visceral sense by the characters' struggles in life that somehow reflect the reader's,
3. Cheer for the characters who overcome their flaws, have evolved, and have reached their goals, perhaps causing the reader to re-consider his own.

(29)

USE YOUR WRITER'S POWER:

1. What do you want your reader to <u>learn</u> from your characters?
2. What do you want your reader to <u>feel</u> from experiencing the characters' lives through their eyes?
3. How do you want your reader to *think* differently?

The Power of the Writer:

1. Can change the way people *think* by giving the reader a glimpse of life through the characters' eyes,
2. May allow the reader to imagine how it would *feel* to see life through the character's eyes,
3. Can offer your readers a message you want them to walk away with.

(30)

PUBLISHING APPROACHES (MORE LATER):

Traditional publishing (slow):

1. Agents: some publishers won't even consider "agent-less writers", but agents cost money. They each specialize in certain genres. Their job is to get you noticed (that will be your biggest hurdle, whether you have written a great book or not),
2. Query letters; sell a book idea in one page or less - synopsis and promotional letter – don't oversell. This is the introduction of you and your book to a traditional publisher,
3. Publishers: you send a synopsis of your book - five pages or less. *They pay you. You don't pay them.* They buy rights to your book,
4. Be forewarned: this process will likely take years,
5. Read as many books on these topics as possible. See suggestions in the **Resources** list in Appendix B.

Traditional publishing is now often eclipsed by self-publishing or hybrid publishing, that is, authors who pursue self-publishing and traditional publishing concurrently.

Self-publishing (fast):

1. You publish and market your own book independent of traditional publishers, agents, and perhaps, even editors (sometimes the latter is a mistake),
2. This is more work for you as an author, but you retain more control (and more opportunities to screw up),
3. Self-publishing requires the author to acquire many skills beyond writing. I offer useful tips for you on this topic later.

Self-publishing is not for everyone, but if you are willing and able to approach your writing as an independent business, you may just snag greater success more quickly than with the traditional publishing approach.

(31)

MARKETING YOUR BOOK (MORE LATER):

1. You likely will establish a presence via blogging and social media (Facebook, Twitter…),
2. You will need your own author website,

3. Consider studying and implementing more advanced marketing techniques: your email list, email campaigns, book signings (once you have a print book in hand), cross-promotions, list swaps, etc.

STARTER NETWORKING RESOURCES (MORE LATER):

1. Online writing groups
2. Local writing groups

STARTER WRITING REFERENCES – BOOKS AND WEB SITES (MUCH MORE LATER):

1. *Daily Writing Tips* **http://www.dailywritingtips**,
2. **Story Engineering** by Larry Brooks – Mastering the six core competencies of successful writing (Google "Story Engineering" for free downloads, worksheets, etc.),
3. **Structuring Your Novel** by K.M. Weiland – Essential Keys for Writing an Outstanding Story. Weiland has an informative blog and web site. Be sure to follow her at **http://www. helpingwritersbecomeauthors.com/**
4. **The Way of Story** by Catherine Ann Jones – the craft and soul of coverage. Jones is an award winning screenwriter whose credits include "The Christmas Wife" and "Touched by an Angel."
5. **Wired for Story** by Lisa Cron – The writers' guide to using brain science to hook readers from the very first sentence.

5

A PROCESS FOR INSPIRATION

~

Reading happens before writing.

> "If you want to be a writer, you must do two things above all others: *read a lot and write a lot.* There's no way around these two things that I'm aware of, no shortcut." —Stephen King

So in addition to studying books and articles on the craft of writing, I:

- _Read_ a lot of ebooks or paperbacks of my favorite genre, other genres too, and I study their book covers noting how successful authors design their covers,
- _Highlight_ wondrous words, fascinating phrases, odd occupations, inspired ideas for plots, settings, characters (protagonists, antagonists, walk-ons, comic relief…), curious quotes and story ideas (both in ebooks and paperbacks), tropes (recognizable story elements that enable reader familiarity and comfort)…
- Periodically _enter_ all of these highlighted and jotted notes into my **_Idea Factory (I.F.)_**, a concept inspired by James Scott Bell. For me, this is a Scrivener project (a single computer file - see next chapter) containing all categories listed above,
- _Review_ the I.F. frequently as an important component of my workflow to seek relevant inspiration for current or future works in progress (WIPs). Every author always banks a few WIPs or needs an occasional kick in the literary derrière.

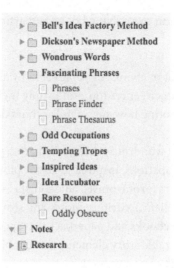

My own **Idea Factory** *implemented in a Scrivener project (accessed via a single file on my computer, also accessible from the cloud, on my tablet or phone). This project grows as I grow as a writer. I.F. attribution: James Scott Bell.*

A unique Idea Factory category - **The Idea Incubator**: I peruse various information sources and record ideas for later consideration within this category to ensure a tried and proven idea maturation process:

- Scan *media* (the news, TV shows, podcasts et al are terrific sources for ideas),
- List *occupations* (you do *what* for a living?),
- Borrow *old plots* (note which genres use what tropes, themes or symbols),
- Ideas for compelling *characters* from real-world observations (details!),
- Predict *trends* (don't just follow them),
- Burning *issues* (what do I feel strongly about?),
- Possible *Book Titles* (those worthy of marinating),
- *First lines* ("It was the best of times, it was the worst of times, it was the age of wisdom, it was the age of foolishness…" —Charles Dickens),
- Possible *reader magnets* (ideas for giveaways to motivate reader subscriptions to my email list. This book is one of my reader magnets that emerged from my *idea incubator*),
- Compelling *content* (what grabs *me* will also grab my readers).

Worthy ideas get *promoted* through various stages of incubation:

- *Back burner* (an idea must start somewhere),
- *Front burner* (I promote the best ideas from the back burner with more detail),
- *White hots* (up from the front burner, but with even more well-crafted thought),
- *Serious book ideas* (the white hots to which I might commit a month or many months to create a full-fledged story's first draft).

With this process, when I finish a book or a series, I will have already teed up several highly qualified candidates for my next project. I'll then need to decide *why* I want to write that next book before committing to the project, and for *whom* (the *"Five Ws"* we discussed in **Chapter 3.** With that in mind, I'll decide either to:

- Write to market *demand* (per Chris Fox), or
- Write for personal *passion* (with no profit motive), or…

The next section will get us writing!

6

A SEVEN-STEP WRITING WORKFLOW

～

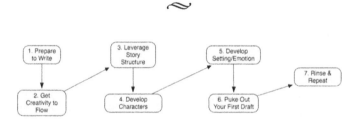

A simple 7-step process for writing your novel (this diagram created by a useful little program called Scapple from the same company that produces Scrivener).

1. WRITING PREPARATION:

- Understand what you're writing and why (see **Chapter 3**),
- What's your definition of success and who is your *ideal reader? Specifically? This is critical!*
- Where will your book fit into the eco-system (where would you place it on a bookstore shelf)? If

you don't know, you haven't yet identified your genre, sub-genre and your ideal reader,

- Try to model your book after similar best-sellers (cover, title, sub-title, blurb, back cover text, tropes, mood…). This is not the place to get overly creative unless you don't care about sales. This is about meeting reader expectations, and *then* exceeding them once they're fans. See Chris Fox's **Write Fast, Write Smarter Series** in the resource list in **Appendix B**,

2. GET YOUR CREATIVE MOJO WORKIN':

Feel free to review my process for inspiration in **Chapter 5**. Now snag the "sparks," like capturing fireflies in a bottle, wherever you are. Carry a small pocket size notebook, smartphone and/or a voice recording device. Otherwise, delicious details are too easily lost:

- Start compiling your research *long before you start writing* (consider doing so in your *Idea Factory*—remember?), but even as you launch a new project, more ideas will *continue* to flow. *Do not let them escape either!*
- Some like a tool called **EverNote** – useful *and free on one device* (fee versions are also available where multiple devices sync with each other). Capture prose, photos (to use as you think of describing a character or a setting), diagrams, lists, maps, etc. with your narrative to explain each, all kept in

single *note* if you wish. Share documents between reviewers (premium plan), including to-do lists,

- You should also look at other apps like **Notion, Clickup, Workflowy,** etc. All vary in learning curves, ancillary features that focus on collaboration with others, project management capabilities, etc. Each also requires a learning curve.
- In general, I recommend any simple note-taking app to capture ideas *anywhere and anytime*. Best if it (or another app) also offers voice recording capability for snagging voice notes.
- I like and use **Apple Notes**. This **simple** *free* note-taking app is automatically included on all my Apple devices. Easy. Fast. Auto-syncs across my phone, tablet (iPad) and computers (Mac & MacBook), I can draw simple diagrams, make nested lists—including to-do lists—I can incorporate photos, voice notes… Did I mention simple, as in a no-brainer to learn and use? So if you're using Apple devices, this is my recommendation.
- There is likely an analogous app on Android devices.

Once you've decided on a general concept for your book, decide what tool(s) beyond simple note-making you'll use to structure your long-form project (not-so-short story, novella, novel, memoir…).

Some prefer to use *MicroSoft Word*, which is fine, but you can do better (opinion). *Word* is a decent word processor, but it is not optimized for long-form projects.

Through trial and error, I found I favor the following two robust *organizational tools* (software) that will advance your writing skills while they help you organize your writing projects and keep track of myriad details, like they do for me:

Outlining Your Novel (OYN) Workbook Software:

OYN runs on MacOS or PC Windows (a $40 one-time price at the time of this writing). Use it over and over again—like a member of your staff. This simple but useful program offers hundreds of incisive "what-if" questions and imagination-revving exercises. This fun resource features a well-structured interface that will show you how to:

- Create your own personalized outlining (idea structuring) process,
- Brainstorm premise and plot ideas,
- Flesh out your characters with in-depth "interview" questions for each,
- Choose and create the right settings (venues), and
- Organize your scenes.

More like a sketch of your book than a traditional outline, by using *OYN software*, you will get lots of ideas to help you create a *premise* (a few paragraphs) or a *synopsis* (a few pages) that describes your complete novel along with a scene list that you can drop into *Scrivener*. That's next, because *OYN* is not really a word processor. Nor is it intended to organize long-form prose. Scrivener most definitely is. K.M. Weiland offers **an accompanying book to the OYN software** (optional and purchased separately) that I found useful and insightful.

Some prefer a similar tool called **Plottr** ($25 annually or $99 lifetime) which focuses more on visual plot lines and heavily overlaps with Scrivener features (see below). So *Plottr* is more expensive than *OYN* and is redundant with *some Scrivener* functions, but it also integrates better with (integrates into) Scrivener than OYN.

You can find various other programs, some are even free, but they didn't fit my needs. Some assume you already have created your book's premise and provide no help in creating that all-important early project element. Some are broad-based tools that don't help you laser focus on the early part of the writing process. And some focus on collaborative workflows that are more useful to teams, less so for individual authors flying solo. You can follow my lead, or do your own research.

I prefer *OYN*. It is simple, cheap and is a precise tool focused on getting me started on a new project quickly.

Pro tip: *Writing a long-form project requires you to keep track of hundreds or thousands of details. Whatever you decide is right for you, I strongly suggest enlisting the support of author-focused software that supports your own process for developing your characters, settings, actions, relationships and story structure.*

Scrivener Organizational Software

Scrivener runs on MacOS or PC Windows ($49 on-time charge) and also on my iPhone. Android too, I believe. It syncs easily across devices. Plus I automatically back up all my projects to **DropBox** in the cloud.

Where *OYN* and similar programs get you started in defining the very early stages of a long-form project like a novel, Scrivener helps you keep track of all that as well as all of your research for a project in one place—a single computer file for each project. It exceeds *MS Word* or any other program as a word processor, and it does so much more, all specifically for authors.

I've written ten books (see this book's **Introduction**), countless short stories, articles and blog posts, created my *Idea Factory* (see **Chapter 3**), and more with *Scrivener* so far.

Scrivener requires a bit of a learning curve over *MS Word*, but is *so worth it.* This amazing program saves me a *lot* of time and frustration. I used just the capabilities I needed early on, and I learned its capabilities beyond its superior word processor functions (most of which are virtually identical to *Word)* as I needed them or discovered them. Or if you wish, take a *Scrivener* class. There are several available.

Most serious authors use *Scrivener.* I never took a class and just used what I needed, learning as I went. There are helpful groups on Facebook to assist. Your mileage may vary,

Once I've used *OYN* to create and structure my premise and scene list, *Scrivener* unites everything I need to write, research, and arrange long documents within this single, powerful app. One drawback is the lack of integration between *OYN* and *Scrivener,* but I just cut and paste from one to the other which works well and goes fast.

At its heart, *Scrivener* offers a simple ring-binder metaphor that allows you to gather your material and flick between different parts of your manuscript, notes, images, diagrams and research references with ease:

- Start with your text in manageable sections (scenes, chapters, parts…) of any size, all within a single computer file (a project) and leave *Scrivener* to stitch them together,
- Shuffle, merge, or separate sections within the binder at will. This allows for incredible creative freedom,
- Integrated tools let you plan everything first and restructure later,
- The ***corkboard view*** presents an elegant visual for outlining or for seeing only the synopses of each scene or chapter,
- The ***outline view*** allows you to assign an author-created status to each element of your manuscript, presents a variety of word-count options, etc.,
- The ***scrivenings view*** enables to see and edit all the pieces (scenes, chapters, parts…) as one integrated manuscript. This is very useful for evaluating your scene and chapter transitions, for continuity, and for finding plot holes or other discontinuities. Don't worry about all that just yet, but it's all literally jut one click away when you're ready to use it,
- And as your project grows, Scrivener grows with it. Keep everything for your project (i.e., your novel) in one file on your computer, including all your research, reference images, web links, your premise, copyright info, acknowledgments page, introduction, as well as your scenes and chapters—all neatly organized. *I cannot emphasize enough the importance of this single-file project structure to the serious author, especially with many books in the backlist, and many more in process,*

- *Scrivener* even includes some decent (but rudimentary) manuscript formatting for output to print-on-demand vendors or for <u>easy</u> export to more sophisticated formatting tools like *Vellum* (more on this later).
- There are many other such programs, some are even free, but *OYN* and *Scrivener* together are inexpensive and are the best for my own writing workflow.
- I use Vellum as my formatting software, and it works nicely with *Scrivener*. But *Vellum* only runs on Mac, not a PC. There is a new product that purports to incorporate both Scrivener and *Vellum* (organizing and formatting) capabilities that runs on any platform. It is called **Atticus**, and is worth researching.

3. WRITE A STORY, NOT JUST WORDS:

You should now have seen some familiar concepts presented from different perspectives. That means you're beginning to think like a writer and are becoming more knowledgeable. You have seen some of the following concepts presented at a higher level earlier in this book, but remember I promised you we'd drill down as we progressed. If you're still with me, congratulations. It's time to further enhance your learning experience.

Think about why you love your favorite books (these offer important clues for your own writing):

- How do they begin and end?
- Why must you keep turning pages?
- Why do you crave these books?

Understand the <u>basics</u> of story structure and story checkpoints:

Act I

- Your characters' "<u>Ordinary World</u>" and "The <u>Hook</u>"… offer up your character's *internal* fear plus their *external* conflict,
- <u>Inciting Incident</u>… what draws your hero into the story?
- <u>Act I climax</u> (<u>first plot turning point</u>).

Act II

- Approximately twice as long as Acts I or III, this is the dreaded "Middle," where keeping readers engaged can be challenging,
- <u>Rising action, obstacles, try/fail cycles</u>,
- <u>Midpoint</u> (mirror moment where your key characters ponder their position in the story). Entire books explore this point in any story. For example, see James Scott Bell's book, *"Writing Your Novel from the Middle"* in the Resource list in **Appendix B**. I found this book to be an excellent resource,

- Act II climax (second plot turning point - here it can't get any worse, or so it seems).

Act III

- The Big Climax (final confrontation),
- Denouement or resolution (return to the real world, rounds up loose ends).

Seek out books on the topic of story structure to better understand this all-important topic. You'll find countless insights in the coming chapters and among the resources listed in **Appendix B**. I particularly enjoyed reading ***Beginnings, Middles and Ends*** by Nancy Kress.

4. WRITE A CHARACTER THAT PEOPLE WILL WANT TO SPEND TIME WITH:

- Use just one main character (MC), at least early in your career as a novelist,
- Reader must *really care* about your MC,
- This will also shape the Point of View (POV) of your narrative (i.e., first-person, third-person, present tense, past tense...)
- What does s/he want and why? What/who stops him/her?

- How does your MC overcome <u>obstacles</u> along the way?
- How does the journey change your character? This is called a character's <u>arc</u> which can go in a positive or negative direction. If neutral, that's static and perhaps less interesting.

5. WHAT HAPPENS, WHY AND WHERE:

- Use <u>setting</u> and <u>emotion</u> to bring <u>conflict</u> to your <u>plot</u>,
- Develop specific and compelling <u>settings</u> where each scene in your story takes place. Your readers must clearly see these settings in their mind's eye. This means you must incorporate plausible detail into your settings. Remember how we recorded details from real life by taking *explicit* notes earlier in this chapter?

6. INITIALLY, JUST GET WORDS ONTO THE PAGE:

- Unlike talking, you get to revise (<u>edit</u>) what you have to say in a book,
- *"The <u>first draft</u> of anything is shit!"* —Ernest Hemingway,
- *But* you can't <u>edit</u> a blank page,
- Schedule your <u>writing time</u> like you schedule any other important activity,
- Use focused, timed writing and set <u>word-count goals</u>—see the Chris Fox books in the resources list in the **Appendix B** for valuable tricks and exercises to flex your literary muscles.

7. WRITING IS REWRITING (EDITING):

- Start with *self-editing.* Print out or view in different formats and edit at least twice. Use your brain and some editing tools. I'll offer some specific recommendations later,
- Optionally use a *professional editor,* a person who will charge a few hundred to a few thousand dollars per manuscript, but for that, you get a lot. We'll also discuss more affordable options in the coming chapters. But for all of these options, you need to be aware of the types of editing services serious authors employ. Yup, keep reading…

There are at least three types of edits:

a. *Story* (content) edits – the most important and the most expensive:

- Also called a *developmental edit.*
- Is your story structure working?
- Are characters engaging?
- Are there plot holes (specific story elements that don't make sense)?
- Is there continuity and flow between sub-plots?

b. *Line* edits - just the essentials, but cheaper:

- Also called the red pen approach (misspellings, etc.).
- Then you'll need to perform more rewrites based on these edits. Just do it, or you'll look like a rank amateur.

c. _Proofreading_ - the most basic type of editing and easiest to find free:

- Typos, grammatical errors.

Get started _today!_

For more insights on editing and tools to ease the journey, see **Chapter** 7. In other words, turn the page.

7

A SYSTEMATIC APPROACH TO CREATIVITY

WHY IS THIS DARN PAGE STILL BLANK?

Remember, inspiration comes from:

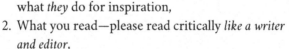

1. Talking with other more experienced writers— what *they* do for inspiration,
2. What you read—please read critically *like a writer and editor,*
3. What you observe and capture—pay attention to the world around you.

HOW DO YOU EVOLVE FROM A ROUGH DRAFT TO THE WELL-WRITTEN PAGE?

1. Never stop learning about the craft of writing–and don't wait to start writing until you *know it all,* or you'll never start,
2. Besides, writers are proud of how much their writing improves from early work to later work – start the journey now and start growing as a writer,
3. Show your pride by writing *every day,* at least for a few minutes, starting *today*.

All of the above, plus:

1. Find, read and take notes from articles, books and web sites that offer insights into bolstering your weakest skills. Then immediately practice writing with your new insight,
2. My own best treasure trove of materials are often found online and in used book stores. I'm cheap,
3. I pillage my used books on writing, brutally dog-earring pages, highlighting, jotting notes in paper notebooks, in my *Idea Factory* or in my *Notes* app. Then I donate those books to the next RV park's lending library (most of them, anyway), or I donate them to the used book store in the next town we visit,
4. Get a mentor. Or six. How? Just ask! Good writers love to help other writers improve. Great writers insist on it. Just remember that the really good writers are busy, so respect their time and they'll

respect you with a few invaluable pearls of wisdom now and then.

Self-Editing Resources

After you've completed your first draft (your initial quick writing, end-to-end), you will need to clean up your manuscript. That's where the editing process comes in. So let's  drill down on that aspect of your process. Many writers dread editing. Learn to enjoy that part of the process. I do so with some very cool tools.

For self-editing, you should employ strong writer's tools that check what you've written for proper grammar, diction, readability and style.

 Why use editing tools (software)? Because you and I don't know what we don't know, of course!

Such tools not only offer you priceless learning opportunities, though there will be considerable overlap between these tools, they all make editing less dreary:

1. *Good*: **The Hemingway App** runs on Macs and PCs (free online, but offline = $19.99 one-time). *Hemingway* features a beautiful user interface. A simple but good app, especially for beginners! I'm prone to *purple prose* (overly flowery language), and *Hemingway* regularly kicks my butt. The program's editing engine emulates Earnest Hemingway's minimalistic style – be careful here – it can go too

far. Turns out my own choice of authorial voice is not *that* minimalistic. The app definitely opened my eyes, though! Worth owning. You'll want this app in your tool kit.

2. *Better*: **Grammarly**'s free version is far superior to rudimentary grammar checkers in most word processors (e.g., *MS Word*). *Grammarly* provides nice explanations of each correction suggested so you know *why* a change is offered (learning opportunities) before you click to accept or reject a recommended change. With heavy overlap with the next tool, I suggest you try the free web version for a while, and then promote yourself to the next tool I'll discuss and recommend.

3. *Best*: **ProWritingAid.** You'll find the free online version useful but limited (only processes 500 words at a time that you cut 'n paste). I use the premium version at $79 per year. *PWA* also offers a lifetime license for $400. Look for periodic sales offers, usually near year-end. *PWA* is a very powerful and effective tool, but is slightly less easy to use than *Grammarly*. **PWA is my favorite robot "writing coach."** They offer a one-time free trial on your complete manuscript – use it wisely. I wrote a review of PWA a while back. Its relatively painless integration with *Scrivener* is a wonderful productivity aid in my workflow. Check out my review at **https://genowrites.wordpress.com/2018/02/23/authors-checklist-prowritingaid/**. Please note that I was using the free online cut 'n paste version of PWA when I wrote this review, but beyond that, its function is identical to the premium version which requires no cutting or pasting.

4. *Sophisticated:* **Autocrit.** At $30/month, it is costly, but is arguably the most powerful editing tool. It analyzes and recommends expert changes based on your word choice, your strong suits (or lack thereof), dialogue advice, pacing and momentum. *Autocrit* then compares your prose to best-sellers' published works in various genres. I couldn't justify the expense. Besides, I believe PWA offers everything I need.

5. Choose your tools and courses. Read **https://thewritelife.com/tools-for-writers/** for some useful comparisons of editing and coaching software.

Other editing resources:

1. Here is a good article on **Punctuation, e.g., in dialogue**: http://theeditorsblog.net/2010/12/08/punctuation-in-dialogue/

2. Take full advantage of free blog articles and newsletters, like **Jane Friedman's Electric Speed:** https://www.janefriedman.com/free-newsletter/

3. **A Novel Edit** at https://anoveledit.com/ is a professional editing service (there are lots from which to choose).

A SENSE OF PURPOSE

 Writing daily gives me a daily sense of purpose.

Having written my own story first (see **Chapter 3**), and by referring to it periodically, I command a clear vision in my mind. I know who I am as a writer and what I aim to achieve.

That story remains a visible reminder in what I call my *author journal*. This is a notebook into which I record daily entries. I *always* take a little time to date and record my activities as a serious author in at least two of the following six categories each day:

- *Writing (**W**):* Includes editing. See **Chapter 4**,
- *Reading (**R**)*: See **Chapter 5**,
- *Idea Factory (**I**)*: See **Chapter 5,** also **Chapter 6** and **Chapter 7**,
- *Author Biz (**B**)*: Accounting, direct sales, website maintenance. See **Chapter 13**,
- *Marketing (**M**)*: See **Chapter 13** & **Chapter 14**,
- *Learning (**L**)*: Topics and sources related to the craft of writing. See **Appendix B**

Yes, we're building on what you've already read or have yet to read in this book.

By maintaining this journaling practice, I keep reminding myself I am serious about my writing. Even this little bit of structure in my day as a writer reminds me of my purpose: I *am* an author, I *have* a purpose, and I *need* to honor that purpose. *Daily.*

To illustrate, allow me to share a couple of recent entries from my *author journal* with you (it's always open on my desk as a constant reminder):

- 4/2 - **M**: Sell paperbacks (DD, FD) at BSM Farmer's Market; **W**: edit *Why Write? Why Publish?* Add Appendix A. **B:** update sales/expense spreadsheet from today's sales. **R**: continue reading Kristen Hannah's *Four Winds* (research for *Jake's Flame*). **M:** consider new title: *Black Blizzard* instead of *Jake's Flame*.
- 4/3 - **L**: Study content of Author Imprints' *AuthorPro Newsletter*; **B**: sign up as an IndieBound.org affiliate. Add 2 new email subscribers to AWeber (see **Chapter 14**) from yesterday. **M**: outline early draft of monthly newsletter to subscribers. **R/L**: read David Wyatt's *New Essays on The Grapes of Wrath* (research for *Jake's Flame* - see **Appendix A**).

Note: my actual entries are more brief and cryptic, but I've expanded them here for illustrative purposes. *I make it a priority to hit at least two of the six categories daily which yields a certain sense of accomplishment and focus.* This takes only a minute or three each day, but I find this to be an invaluable discipline.

Pro tip: *I envision some day my author journal might come in* *handy with the IRS as I seek to deduct my author business expenses from my tax burden (should I get audited - consult your own tax professional). For the same reason, I employ a time keeper app to record my time spent on various author business tasks that consume my time. I use Punch Time Clock on my iPhone, and then weekly I upload this timekeeping data to a spreadsheet on my desktop computer, an iMac (I use an open-source, aka free, spreadsheet program from OpenOffice.org). That is essentially identical to MS Excel.*

SEEKING HELP FROM OTHER AUTHORS:

Attend webinars, writing conferences, subscribe to educational web sites:

1. Free seminars,
2. Free webinars (Internet- or web-based seminars) and online writer's education– Google "free writing webinars." There are a lot.

Google "**writers conferences.**" They can be educational but expensive (conference fees, travel, lodging…). These are excellent opportunities to network with other writers, literary agents, editors, publishers, and to attend seminars. Many now offer online alternatives (a response to COVID).

Subscribe to various writing groups:

1. **Helping Writers Become Authors**
2. **Writer's Digest Free Webinars**
3. **Kindlepreneur**
4. **The Creative Penn**
5. **Writers Helping Writers**

6. Not-free stuff on the **Writers Digest** web site – they have some free stuff but also many wonderful offerings with a price tag.

Join online writer's *critique groups. This is important*:

1. You critique (crit) other writers' unpublished works to earn points. Et voilá! You're a *critter!*
2. Then you spend accumulated points you've earned when you post your own work for a crit by others, usually a few chapters at a time. You may receive several crits at a time, and in this way, you may also find *beta readers* (more on this later), maybe even fans,
3. Be prepared to receive brutal critiques of your own work and be ready to accept them gracefully and constructively. That's how you grow as a writer. That is exactly what you want. You will likely not get that caliber of candor from friends and relatives,
4. If you just want someone to fawn over every precious word you've stabbed with the end of your quill, ask Aunt Alice ("that's nice, dear!" and kiss your Pulitzer, Pushcart or Hugo bye-bye),
5. Watch for critters who know what they're doing with in-depth critiques that are thorough, helpful and insightful. Then check out *their* work to return the favor. Fair is fair. If you like what you see, ask them to exchange entire manuscripts with you (*off-group*). Easy. And what a great way to network with other writers—by scratching each others' backs!

So if you want to grow as a writer and learn as a critter, check out:

1. **Critique Circle** (one of my favorites – free or fee),
2. **Internet Writing Workshop** (more complex email-based site). Read how one author successfully navigated IWW: **Meg Wesley on IWW full novel critiques** at http://megwestley.blogspot.com/2009/12/writing-critique-groups-i-internet.html
3. Your local writers' groups (ask around),
4. Check local colleges and libraries,
5. Use your favorite search engine!

8

MOST COMMON MISTAKES

WHY YOU MIGHT BE USING TOO MUCH
DESCRIPTION:

1. You aren't trusting your readers to *get it*,
2. You love your story details too much,
3. You're still growing your story sensibilities.

**The two most common areas to look for too much
description:**

1. Character description:

- *Face*: be brief! "I'd heard you were handsome. You're not. But your face is interesting."
- *Hair*: be brief! "His tousled red mop bobbled as he spoke."
- *Eye color*: intimate detail only. "Her chocolate eyes…"
- *Body*: not detail, but stature. "This aging chunk of granite towered over me…"
- *Clothes*: early on to set the stage, then not so much. Dress is only important in a story when it is important to the character.
- *Scars/Special Features*: do they matter to the story? Otherwise, what's the point?
- As seen by other characters? Protagonist? Yes. Others? Not so much. Particularly *cringe-worthy*, "she observed herself in the mirror!" Yuck. This is strictly amateur hour,
- Describe only details that matter to the character *in the moment* and not contrived.

2. Description of settings:

- Find the perfect place to put the details,
- Descriptions only matter when readers *need* them,
- At the beginning of the book, use just enough detail to orient readers—within the scene and for the overall story world,
- Then sow additional details *as they become pertinent,*
- At the beginning of a scene, or at a chapter break, reorient readers, *but* is the setting the most important part of the scene? If so, open with it, relevant to its scope of importance. If not, hold back a little. Introduce the scene hook, sketch a few setting details, then slowly dole out other

pertinent descriptors as they become necessary (as characters begin to interact with them),

- For already familiar settings, the only details you need to repeat are *new* details,
- When detail is necessary for complex settings, share all important details with readers, but do it artfully. Sprinkle them into the action of the plot and development of the characters,
- Make all the details you share *matter* to the story – make them mean more than just words about brick and mortar.

Learning the art of avoiding too much description is ultimately the art of *controlling your narrative*.

- When you move past description as merely *description* and bring it into play as a technique for advancing plot, character, and theme through the judicious choice of details, you will raise the entire tenor of your book.

9

THE EDITOR'S APPROACH

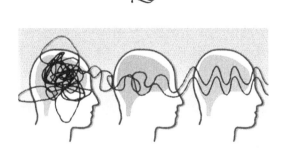

You've written your story. Maybe you exercised the seven-step approach in **Chapter 4**. But after all that, if you haven't hired a professional editor, which can be costly, there is still more you can do yourself to further polish your precious manuscript.

Enter Shawn Coyne's **Story Grid methodology**. In fact, you can benefit from reviewing these story grid resources before you begin writing too, but if it stands in the way of banging out your first draft, you can always benefit from this hard-core editor's perspective later, for your next project (downloadable tools, podcasts, articles, mini-courses). Shawn is a storied editor with decades of big-house publishing experience.

But do not let this approach confuse you or sway you from the basic but all-important three-act story structure example we reviewed in **Chapter 6**. Story grid can be very useful as another way of structuring scenes or thinking about your writing. This methodology can also be useful for fitting your story within what works for specific genres, and what doesn't.

Bottom line: **whatever is useful to *you* is what you should stick with.**

The nucleus of the story grid is pretty straightforward. I keep a post-it note on my computer. It looks like this:

THE STORY GRID SCENE STRUCTURE (EVERY SCENE):

1. Inciting Incident
2. Progressive Complications
3. Crisis
4. Climax
5. Resolution

This scene structure also applies well at a broader level to your entire manuscript; hence, the *grid* moniker.

James Scott Bell, famed international thriller author and author of the #1 bestseller for authors, **"Plot & Structure,"** offers another simple but valuable approach to analyzing your own scenes—the *molecules* of your story, each one critically important to the whole story *organism*. You'll also find the checklist below on a "sticky note" stuck to the front my computer monitor so I see it every time I sit down to write. I find this one resonates best with me:

SCENE CHECKLIST (PER JSB):

- Memorable setting,
- Characters/goals,
- Conflict (frustrated desire),
- Movement (physical, story…)
- Vital/exciting,
- Stakes (higher is usually better),
- Events/action,
- Character reacts (to events),
- New info (or selectively reiterate old),
- Leads to next scene
- SUES (something unexpected in every scene)

If you find you like JSB, and are interested in the finer points of plot and structure, I recommend another insightful book of his called "**Write Your Novel From The Middle.**" Yet another way to view your writing method. A fascinating premise.

And another useful resource from a brilliant young man named Derek Murphy: his "**How to Self-Edit Your Book**" course. He is improving this *free* course, and it will ultimately cost $49. He also recommends many of the same books I recommend. If you haven't been exposed to Derek, turn up the volume and hang on!

10

MORE ADVANCED STORY STRUCTURE

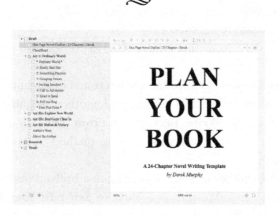

I've mentioned Derek Murphy before. A delightful young man—the ultimate author road warrior—who once reserved a castle in Europe for one of his writing classes. He's as authentic as they come, and offers a plethora of both free and paid resources for writers.

I now leverage an extremely useful resource from Derek —his comprehensive ***FREE 24-chapter-novel Scrivener*** *template* (a fill-in-the-blanks "form") that is simple, instructive *and* remarkable. This template, which requires the phenomenal *Scrivener* software, an invaluable productivity tool for authors (see **Chapter 6**), guides you through creating a novel in the following tried-and-proven format. You can find Derek's brilliant free template at https://www.creativin die.com/free-novel-outlining-template-for-scrivener/

At the beginning of each chapter, each of which is a story structure checkpoint within the template, Derek provides specific and helpful guidance for that chapter and for each major story element (inciting incident, first plot point, etc). From there, you create a scene list and start filling in the blanks. Download the chapter list below as a "Cheat Sheet" infographic from Derek's site at the web link above if you wish, but you'll find a mini-tutorial of each story checkpoint in his free *Scrivener* template:

Act I - Hero and Ordinary World (chapters 1-6):

- Really bad day,
- Something peculiar,
- Grasping at straws,

* Inciting Incident,

- Call to adventure,
- Head in sand,
- Pull out the rug,

* First Plot Point,

Act IIA - Exploring New World (chapters 7-12):

- Enemies & allies,
- Games & trials,
- Earning respect,

First Battle

- Forces of evil,
- Problem revealed,
- Truth & ultimatum,

Midpoint,

Act IIB - Bad Guys Close In (chapters 13-18):

- Mirror stage,
- Plan of attack,
- Crucial role,

Second Battle,

- Direct conflict,
- Surprise failure,
- Shocking revelation,

Second plot point,

Act III - Defeat & Victory (chapters 19-24)

- Giving up,
- Pep talk,
- Seizing the Sword

* Final Battle,

- Ultimate defeat,
- Unexpected victory,
- Bittersweet return,

* *Rebirth*

I **love** using this template within *Scrivener*! This has distilled the wisdom of hundreds of successful writers to a simple outline that works. The template is instructional, easy to understand, helps organize an entire project within a single computer file, and I use this template within *Scrivener* synchronized across my Mac, iPad and iPhone, as well as an automated backup in the cloud via DropBox. A *Windows* version of *Scrivener* is available too.

11

THE SUBTLETY OF SUBTEXT

~

'Fortunately, the blood splatters had not obscured the circled text.

A powerful technique so artfully described by Charles Baxter in his masterwork, **"The Art of Subtext: Beyond Plot,"** requires some practice, but every serious writer knows how powerful this technique can be. That's why *subtext* commands its own chapter here.

This is a more advanced writing technique, but one well-worth mastering.

Problem: too little description:

A scene with decent dialog but with little or no mention of *setting* is often referred to as the *vanishing scene:*

1. Readers have no idea *where* the characters are,
2. Readers are offered no imagery of *what* the setting looks like,
3. Because of little or no setting description, the reader has no idea of the characters' interactions with the setting.

Solution: flesh out appropriate setting detail:

- Brings our story to life,
- Gives us opportunities to grow closer to our characters and learn more about them as they interact with the setting.

Problem: readers also hate too much description:

- Lengthy descriptions are almost inevitably boring (e.g., *info dumps*),
- Because they don't matter!

Solution: Subtext!

Another reason why too much description pushes readers out of your story? Too much description saps the story of *subtext*:

- Often seems like magic simply because, by its very nature, it is *the execution of the unexplained,*
- It is *supposed* to be invisible. It lives in the shadowy underworld *beneath* our words—the phantom in our opera.

Subtext allows the reader to:

- Ask questions about characters and situations, to fill in blanks, to come to their own conclusions, to exercise their imagination!
- Enables readers to observe and learn *without* being *taught* or *preached to.*

So if *subtext* is largely the science of *what is not,* what the heck **is** *subtext* and how do I (not) write it while writing *with* it?

THE 5 KEYS TO CRACKING *SUBTEXT'S* SECRET CODE (PER CHARLES BAXTER):

1. Story *subtext* arises from the space between two known, fixed points:

- *Subtext* only works when it arises from its context,
- If *subtext* is the shadow behind your story, then there must first be figures standing in the sun casting that shadow,
- Interesting blank spaces can only arise when there are existing shown (not blank) elements of the story,

- Tell readers what they need to know about characters, plot or story world (otherwise, you have no story),
- But you do *not* explain away the spaces in between,
- Because you are resisting the urge to explain everything in between those points, you are allowing them to discover the implicit shape in between.

2. Story *subtext* must explicitly exist beneath the surface:

- *False assumption: subtext* is basically nonexistent. It's a blank space.
- *Subtext* is *very* explicit. It's very real,
- It *must* exist, in the author's intentions and in the story's allusions, if it is to carry any weight,
- Create your story's *subtext* deliberately which requires an absolute understanding of your characters' backstories, motivations, and goals with a firm grip on the world around your characters. This is why getting to know your characters via interviews (see **Chapter 4**) is so vital.

3. Story *subtext* must *remain* under the surface:

- I have to trust the *subtext* to carry itself—which it *cannot* do if I raise it above the surface into context,
- Resist the urge to explain! Especially true of dialogue,
- Make it a habit to force characters into talking *around* subjects or coming at things sidelong or metaphorically,

- It's great restraint shown in stories rich in *subtext* that makes them intellectually stimulating and emotionally moving,
- The one exception to this is important story *revelations,*
- Keep certain aspects of your story (backstory secrets, antagonistic clues, etc.) under the surface for *most* of the story before revealing them in important scenes that advance the plot.

4. Story *subtext* is created by dichotomy or a disparity:

- Fixed points of your story's context seem like they don't *quite* align, and *that* immediately sparks readers' curiosity,
- Note, however, that *subtext* cannot arise from an *explicit* question,
- These dichotomies must remain *implicit* questions when readers are led to believe the truth about a character or a situation that is *different from how it appears on the surface,*
- "It's always great when there can be a definite dichotomy between interior and exterior behavior. Truly that's the heart of *subtext.*" - Joe Long,
- The dichotomy raises questions. Why is this character this way? What is the internal conflict driving these contradictions? And which of these aspects of his nature is the true aspect?

5. Story *subtext* exists in the silent spaces:

- Cultivate your characters' silence. Even when the story requires you to explain certain things to readers, resist the temptation to have your characters spell everything out to *each other,*

- *Do not—repeat, do not—*allow your characters to tell each other exactly what they're thinking,
- Can you rephrase the explicitness of the dialogue to keep some of that iceberg under the water even while sharing necessary information?

Example:

- Too much info = no subtext: *Sarah asked, "Are you a murderer?" to which he responded, "Yes, but only of men."*
- Less info = subtext: *Sarah asked, "Have you ever killed anyone?" to which he only looked at his badly scuffed loafers, but said nothing. Then he stared into her tear-rimmed eyes with a deep sorrow.*

12

DESIGN & FORMAT YOUR BOOK

~

So you've written and edited your masterpiece. Now what? It's time to polish its shine.

FORMATTING AND GRAPHICS SERVICES:

Both text formatting and graphic design will be essential to get your book "print ready." Ebooks too. This is a brief survey of a few useful design and formatting tools. They range from completely DIY (Do-It-Yourself) to partially DIY, to hiring a pro. You can use free tools that require sweat equity or tools that cost some money but streamline the process, potentially saving you hundreds, maybe thousands of hours. I also use some of these to create marketing graphics for social media banners or book advertisements.

First, let's look at a few free graphics services to help you create DIY book covers:

Canva

- They say, "Amazingly Simple Graphic Design Software."
- Lots of free stuff and some for-fee stuff (e.g., high-end templates),
- Good for book cover design and other graphics (templates, posters, logos, blog posts…),
- Works well on desktops and tablets,
- Really easy drag-n-drop interface,
- Easy to share (FB, Twitter...) or download (graphic file, PDF…),
- I've found free Canva services somewhat useful, but chose to use a different service.

Photofunia

- They say, "A free photo editing site packed with a huge library of picture editor effects & photo filters,"
- I use this sparingly for unusual effects (PR images…),
- Good for graphics in blog posts,
- Limited use in my book projects.

Professional Graphics Design

For my first two books, I paid a professional designer to create two print covers, including their ebook counterparts for $400 (**Elisabeth Mackey Graphics Design**). They are beautiful covers, but I knew I could design my own.

DIY Graphics Design

As an example of graphics I produced myself, see the graphic at the beginning of this chapter. I knew this would be more cost effective for the many books I would publish. Plus it was fun!

But this work does require a certain aptitude for the visual arts. If you aren't confident designing your own cover, however, and having a great cover *is* essential, *please* hire a pro. Or take a book cover design course. That's what I did—from Derek Murphy for $27.

I am artistically inclined. At least *I* think I am. Note that while I learned a lot about book cover design from Derek and others, I chose not to use his book cover creator tool—it's just too raw for my purposes. See my alternative recommendations next. More sophisticated graphics programs are not free, but might make sense if you need a lot of graphic design work:

- **Adobe Photoshop & InDesign:** This is considered the gold standard by many professionals, but are also a lot more expensive with a *long and steep* learning curve. $21/month (or as part of Adobe's Creative Cloud—20+ apps=$53/month). I keep an old copy of PS around. Old tools die hard,
- **Bookbrush**: This web-based tool is really simple, chocked full of marketing features (pre-

configured templates for ads, social media, really nice banners and their most popular feature: *instant mock-ups*. Limited free plan, a premium monthly plan ($8.25 to $20.50/month) or their annual subscription ($99 - $246). They have a nice $15/month plan,

- **PicMonkey**: Another great web-based app for designing semi-sophisticated book covers (e.g., this book's cover) or impressive social media banners. $8/month to $80/month. I use the $13/month plan for my book covers (after taking several cover design courses). I use a **KDP cover template** as my base layer for proper book cover dimensions (do *not* resize!).

- I really like both *Bookbrush* and *PicMonkey*. Each has its strengths, but I can't justify the expense of subscribing to both. I chose *PicMonkey* by waiting for their occasional annual subscription discount (about $70).

- **Ingram/Spark** (IS) requires publishers to use their own template (slightly different from KDP's), so I use that for submitting to them. This is a free download, but you need a precise page count and specify type of paper you'll require (cream or white). IS provides great tutorials.

- <u>**Pre-formatted book design templates:**</u> You can also purchase complete downloadable book design templates. This is a hybrid approach. More on this below.

<u>Note</u>: Within both *Bookbrush* and *PicMonkey*, you can create "**brand kits**" (your logo, consistent color palettes, templates, fonts and other graphics to be used for all your campaigns or marketing materials). This makes it simple to

repeatedly return and use this kit to create your consistent brand look 'n feel. We will discuss your author brand later.

BOOK FORMATTING:

- **Objective:** To consistently create an attractive and professional-looking *interior design* for your book.
- **Okay**: Highly manual: *MS Word -> Kindle Direct Publishing* (*KDP* epub file) but time-consuming and error-prone
- **Good**: Book design templates mentioned below.
- **Better**: Simple but efficient formatting via a **Scrivener** export. Extremely generous free trial or a $50 one-time charge to buy,
- **Best**: Very simple and very efficient (the gold standard): *Vellum* isn't cheap, but it makes the most sense if you're going to format more than a few books. ***Vellum** eBooks*: $200 (one-time charge) OR *Vellum Press* ($250 one-time for both ebook and print). Their free trial is full-function *except* no *Generate Books,* a.k.a. *Export with Formatting.* Beautiful page headings, footers, ornamental breaks, one-click to change the style for an entire manuscript. In a word, **awesome!** Example: note the pretty little "ornamental break" at the beginning of every chapter of this book? That's *Vellum.* Same with the right and left justification for paragraphs of text in this chapter, placement and size of images and LOTS more. I export my *Scrivener* manuscript (.docx) directly into Vellum with one click, I command it to create the appropriate formatted print-ready files for Kindle,

Apple Books, Nook, Google Play, Kobo and PDF—all at the same time *with one click.*

- *Pro tip: While Vellum is the gold standard of book formatting, you need an Apple Mac to use it. But if you're on a PC, never fear. You can access a remote Mac that you don't own but can rent time on. Yes, this is an extra process step for PC users, but here's how you get it done: https://paulteague.net/how-to-use-vellum-on-a-pc/. And if you're wondering whether this is worth the extra effort, read this review of a service called MacinCloud: https://skinnerselfpub.com/vellum-software-formatting-for-pc-users/*

- *(Ed: Technology Update - Try Atticus as this new product combines the function of Scrivener and Vellum that runs on any platform - and it is cheaper ($147 as of this update).*

Another alternative: Pre-packaged **Book Design Templates** (not free but affordable at $40/book to $80/multiple books to $150/commercial if you format for other authors). See http://www.bookdesigntemplates.com/?inf_contact_key= 02ec00247adb b1d9725b3b1d8484cf8beef90403f37d5abfc1446cf90e9e6315% 22%20%5Cl%20%22fiction. These templates offer even more customizable interior book designs tailored to a specific genre:

- For *MS Word*, *Pages*, *InDesign*, or easily export from *Scrivener* manuscripts into such a template:
- Format for print and eBook at the same time,
- Designs for fiction and non-fiction, pulp (cheap), inspirational, etc.

- Good if you're only doing one or more books in the same formatted style, but rather expensive if you require several different designs for several books (e.g., one each for science fiction, historical fiction, several non-fiction—cookbooks, travelogues, memoirs…).

13

GET VISIBLE, PUBLISH & SELL

~

I nurture two fiction brands as of this printing, with another on the way (historical crime fiction). Can you see them reflected in my two series? I'm also building a 3rd for my new non-fiction brand in support of authors & independent publishers (UpLife Press is my own publishing company), but to be blunt, I need to listen more to my own advice.

BUILD YOUR OWN AUTHOR *BRAND*

Do not wait until you've finished your first book to nurture your author brand—your very own "platform," that is **your** *unique "look 'n feel." Start NOW!*

Begin with social media (Facebook, Twitter, Instagram…)

1. Talk (a lot) about your passion for writing, but *more importantly,* talk about why anyone should be interested in *you!* ***Sell yourself first, and <u>then</u> your book(s).***
2. What are your passions?
3. What do you spend time doing? That's what you're likely to write about, and that's why your future readers will be interested in what you will (eventually) write about.

Example:

- I like to sail. I have lots of boating friends who watch my social media pages because of our shared interests,
- So for my first book, I decided to write a book about sailing.
- I then pointed to my author website, which contained my boating blog, a book sales link *from my social media pages* where a couple thousand folks were already following me.
- Instant fan base! At least, it's a start.

Entire books provide effective social media strategies,

although this is not my favorite destination as a reader, but an online presence is essential for the independent author and publisher. The two big gorillas are Twitter and Facebook, so that's where I spend some time. **Advanced Twitter Strategies for Authors** written by Ian Sutherland grabbed my attention. Ian's techniques are valid for both fiction and non-fiction:

1. How to attract new Twitter followers,
2. Why becoming an effective influencer on your subject or themes of your books helps you sell more,
3. How to focus your time on Twitter into just fifteen productive minutes per day.

FaceBook (FB) Groups are better for networking and learning, as well as some basic promotion if you don't yet have an ad budget. See **Chapter 14** on marketing. You'll find dozens of helpful writer/author groups to choose, join and contribute to elevate your presence and to expand your awareness of this space so important to your business as an author.

Let's talk about *your* author brand more specifically. I'm still working on mine, but read a great article by Thomas Umstattd Jr. from Author Media, "**10 Classic Branding Blunders Authors Make (and how to avoid them)**" at https://www.authormedia.com/10-branding-blunders-authors-make-and-how-to-avoid-them/

You need a web site, even if it's just a blog. Already have one? That's a good start! *You definitely need an Internet presence that's all yours.* You can start with a free blog hosting site. So if you already have an RV blog, use it to talk about your writing to your RV friends and followers. Hype your site from your FB and Twitter accounts. That's called *directing traffic*.

Several platforms offer free blog hosting:

- **Wordpress.com, Blogspot.com**, there are others...
- Pros and cons to each
- Most have free templates you can use to jump-start your own beautiful site quickly. They make it quite easy to set up simple sites. Plus, it's fun!

Pro tip: *some of these free sites do not allow ads for selling your books.* You might not care right now, but check this out for future reference (or you may need to pay an up-charge to do so).

Keep your website fresh and relevant:

- Add blog posts of interest to your readers at least monthly,
- This is a perfect place to feature your own book(s) with links to the sales pages of your favorite digital store front,
- Later, *or* right away, you might choose to graduate to a specialized or not-free hosting service and possibly premium (not-free) "skins" or templates (some feel these are essential for *serious* authors),

Learn how. Here's a **free tutorial for creating your own author web site** by Joanna Penn at https://www.thecre ativepenn.com/authorwebsite/, who actively empowers *Indie* (independently publishing) authors.

Take a peek at my own author website at **GKJurrens.com.** It's constantly evolving, and that's as it should be. Try different things for your own site to see what works and what doesn't. I'm selling myself <u>and</u> my books! Plus, I make every effort (this takes some time) to prevent *stale content.*

As Joanna says, your author website is your:

- Home base on the Internet,
- The hub for your book(s),
- You can build a site for *free*, but for more control, I use **Bluehost** and **WordPress.org** (different from **Wordpress.com)**. By doing so, I gain more flexibility and a more professional appearance (premium templates, no ads, more options, etc). This approach is not cheap at ~$200 per year, including your own domain name and domain security, which is important), but you likely will score somewhat cheaper promotional pricing for the first year. Since this website is my *headquarters,* this is where I decided to invest some money and time.

Your website is also where you start to build your *email list* of readers, aka *subscribers*. Your subscriber list anchors your entire marketing strategy. See **Chapter 14.** You will find the **Newsletter Ninja** books by Tammy Labrecque and excellent resource to get your email list started.

AWARENESS AND VISIBILITY

To Publish and Sell:

Whether you like "the big gorilla" or not, get to know Kindle Direct Publishing for both your ebooks and print books:

- There is zero upfront cost to publish with KDP,
- KDP is the *big kahuna* with easiest setup, including a book cover creator, free ISBN (book serial number), although there are advantages of buying your own ISBN for each format of each book (ebook + paperback + hardcover +audiobook = 4 ISBNs, all for just one book title), and one ISBN can cost upwards of $100/each, but there are *huge* volume discounts available,
- A good resource for understanding and finding ISBNs is David Wogahn's **Register Your Book.. The Essential Guide to ISBNs, Bar Codes, Copyright and LCCNs,**
- One channel commands the largest audience by far. Further increase your book's visibility with their *Kindle Unlimited,*
- Option: *expanded distribution* (but still under "the big gorilla's" control) and only to other US distributors like Barnes & Noble, Kobo, etc.
- Reality check: it is difficult (time-consuming) to make much money selling books on this number one channel unless you have an ad budget or a large social media/website/email fan base,
- Ads do further increase your book's visibility. I do not recommend them for neophytes. It can be expensive to learn and requires a serious budget for efficacy (with a varying *cost per click*).
- ***Pro Tips:*** *KDP format requirements changed in 2020. They now no longer accept the .mobi file format, but now require a specific epub format). Vellum generates those too. Consider "going wide" for better sales (keep reading).*

Selling outside and independent of just one large channel:

- Options other than the most obvious exist to market and sell your book.
- **BookBaby**: ebook and print. Higher royalties, faster royalty payment to you as an author but not as wide an audience,
- **Lulu**: ebook and print. Smaller audience, generous royalties, specialized support.

"Going Wide"

Aggregators/Distributors: a viable alternative to "you know who" for *going wide* exist for selling across many sales channels:

- **IngramSpark/Lightning Source** (ebooks and print) but they charge for uploads (typically $50 per combined print/ebook title) and revisions (~$25). Lightning Source is a POD vendor, and Ingram/Spark arguably offers the most worldwide sales channels.
- **Smashwords** (eBooks only) was considered the best ebook aggregator/distributor by many authors,
- **Draft-2-Digital** (eBooks only) had fallen out of favor with many authors (disputes over rights, aging technology), but have become the new gold standard since acquiring Smashwords. I use D2D now myself, and love it.
- This landscape changes over time. Be sure to do your own research.

Reader websites for additional visibility (more is better, but each demands an investment of the author's time):

- Think "fan sites,"
- **Goodreads** (very accessible and popular),
- **BookBub** (considered to be the Indie gold standard, but also the toughest to penetrate)…

Sell from your own web site: recommended if you're just starting out:

- It's easiest to just link to online retail stores (digital store fronts) from your own website. Advantage: by directing traffic to your website first, you can offer a signup form to potential email list subscribers before redirecting them to retail sites to buy your book). Disadvantage: you lose influence over potential buyers once they leave your site,
- Set up your own "store" to sell your books directly on your website instead of linking to retail sites. Advantage: you don't share profit (royalties to retailer). Disadvantage: this is not free, is significantly more complex to set up, and you manage your own fulfillment for physical products (shipping, handling, insurance…).
- Read this article to get you started setting up your own store on the world's most popular platform, Wordpress: **The Best WordPress eCommerce Plugins of 2021 Compared.**

Sell your books face-to-face:

- Can be a gratifying experience,
- Work with Indie (Independent) book stores through an organization like **IndieBound.org** as

an affiliate (you scratch their back, they scratch yours).

The All-Important Sales Funnel (SF)

Now here's something I learned after floundering around with my marketing strategy for far too long before finding something that would accomplish the following:

1. How do I deliver my books electronically directly to readers if I just want to give them away to attract subscribers to my email list (aka *reader magnets* that are either temporarily offered free as a promotion, or permanently free, aka *permafree)*? The book you are reading is an example of a reader magnet. I produced it quickly, but it still delivers value and attracts readers to my writing. See Nick Stephenson's free book, **Reader Magnets: Build Your Author Platform and Sell more Books,**
2. How do I build my email list without paying an arm and a leg?
3. How do I gain visibility and sell my books to other authors' fan bases (*email newsletter swaps* and *cross-promotions*)?
4. The type of program that allows this stuff is called a *book funnel*, sometimes also called a *conversion funnel* (as in converting a large number of casual browsers into a smaller number of highly qualified buyers). See David Nadler's book, **The Perfect Conversion Funnel: The Top 9 Funnels Online Experts are Using Today**
5. I gained experience with two such programs that were both affordable and effective. Of course, each have pros and cons. Some authors use both…

BookFunnel:

- <u>Pros</u>: Reasonable cost with a choice of plans ($20/year for a limited plan to $250/year for a robust plan),
- <u>Cons</u>: Not free, and cheapest plan is quite limited in the number of books you can upload and offer to your readers/subscribers.

StoryOrigin:

- <u>Pros</u>: Limited free or robust paid version ($100/year as I'm writing this) which includes email list-building; responsive customer service and very personable (Evan, the developer, is an impressive one-man show). StoryOrigin offers more creative marketing options than BookFunnel as part of its subscription plan.
- <u>Cons</u>: Customer downloading isn't quite as straightforward as *BookFunnel*, but still quite easy.

As an example of the critical value sales funnel offerings provide to my own marketing workflow, I use my equally important email automation service (see **Chapter 14)** to display a subscription form on my website (**GKJurrens.com**) from which I offer potential subscribers the opportunity to receive a free book (a *reader magnet*) in exchange for their email address (their subscription). I'm building my email list while I use *StoryOrigin* or *Book Funnel* to deliver that ebook to them in their preferred format. This requires no intervention from me once I upload the book to the *StoryOrigin* or *Book Funnel* site. They charge nothing on a per title basis within the scope of their plans. These *sales* or *conversion* *funnel* apps even offer my subscribers assistance in down-loading my free book if they need it. Cool, huh?

Now you could perform this service yourself, but fair warning: you do NOT want to be plagued by every other user with questions about whether they want their free book in PDF format, or Kindle format, or some other format. Plus, if a user has problems downloading, do you want to spend your time as a support desk? Or would you rather be writing? Listen to Obi Wan Kenobi… *Use the force, Luke!*

ADVERTISING:

Countless volumes have been written about this, but unless you have a significant budget to burn, approach the topic of paying for advertising (or paying for any service, for that matter) with extreme caution until you have garnered sufficient experience to do so with your eyes wide open.

I strongly recommend focusing on free visibility (social media, etc.) until you have thoroughly studied this topic which is beyond the introductory scope of this book, although Chris Fox offers a nitty gritty book called **Ads for Authors Who Hate Math**.

Suffice it to say here that even with ample savvy and a regular budget to invest, advertising for the neophyte is a roll of the dice. And effective advertising is beyond the scope of most new authors. There is time for tilting this windmill down the road.

14

AUTOMATE YOUR MARKETING

EMAIL MARKETING:

I recommend you investigate support resources to develop your own email list, that is, to collect email addresses of people interested enough in your work to be notified when your next project is available. Think *subscribers.* This is a critical component of your marketing strategy! How do you do that?

Email Marketing Automation (EMA) services

1. I used a premium **AWeber** plan for a year, which was a pleasant but prolonged learning experience. *Aweber Pro* is very robust, but it is not cheap at $19

per month and up for access to their more sophisticated features,

2. I've recently migrated to AWeber's free plan (<500 subscribers), which is quite limited functionally, although it does include strong technical support. Besides, migrating to another EMA platform, while doable, is onerous.

3. One popular alternative is **MailChimp**'s free plan for fewer than 2,000 subscribers. Like most plans, you can upgrade as you grow. See more details below. MC comes highly recommended and is broadly used, but offers no substantive technical support with their free plan other than a plethora of well-written technical articles. I view this as a critical weakness in their free plan.

4. *Pro Tip: Whatever plan you choose, strong technical support is critical unless you are a computer programmer with HTML skills. I am not.*

5. I further suggest you analyze what best fits your own needs, but if you're serious about selling books, **choose one EMA service and get familiar with its use**. Learning and applying this concept took me *months*. **Review this article** which offers you twenty EMA vendors from which to compare and select: https://www.fool.com/the-blueprint/email-marketing-software-reviews/. Then take the time. It's worth it if you're serious about selling books.

6. Don't ignore basic and more advanced email list-building capabilities offered by the sales funnel apps. I'm currently exploring such features within **StoryOrigin** (e.g., group promotions, email list swaps…). I'm looking to augment more full-function EMA capabilities in this way.

To repeat, for EMA rookies, I *strongly* recommend you shop out a basic plan **with technical support** (chat or phone is best, support by email is ok). EMA is not for the feint of heart, but promises big returns *if you stick with it.* I also encourage you to first become familiar with the entire *onboarding process.* For this, I will once again point you toward Tammy Labreque's book, **The Newsletter Ninja** where she guides you to build your email list with a rigorous *onboarding process* (a process to bring new subscribers onboard and to develop a relationship with them strong enough for them to spend money with you). And publishing a newsletter is an integral part of that process.

What does EMA do for you?

A free plan with **MailChimp** (MC), for example, may be a good start for you, but spend some time to learn EMA concepts and to plan your own EMA strategy.

The good news:

1. MC (and most EMA providers) offer a *signup form for your website* so your readers can subscribe. You create this form on MC and embed it in your website, FB, Twitter...
2. *Protects against fake sign-ups and other email scams* through the use of a *double opt-in process.* The subscriber fills in the form on your site with their name and email address. They're then sent a confirmation email within which they click the confirm link, and they're done,

3. The new subscriber sees your prescribed *signup thank you* page,

4. Optional: you send new subscribers a *final welcome email* to further solidify your new relationship,

5. MC has a *simple* sharable form – no HTML (programming) required, but it can be tricky to know where to stuff their HTML code into your site if you're not familiar with such things ("Hello? Tech support? What the heck do I do with this code you provided me?"),

6. *Advanced* customizable forms are available, *but* they require HTML programming experience and a paid subscription,

7. Their *Form Builder* function provides help to design an appropriate signup form to grow your list,

8. You can designate what info you'd like to collect from your subscriber (e.g. zip code, favorite genre, whatever) and which fields are required, etc. Experts agree the less info you request, the more likely you'll get new subscribers.

9. Includes *'unsubscribe' and 'good-bye' email*, or 'forward to a friend'. Pretty comprehensive capability for free!

10. All MC forms are "mobile responsive,"

11. You'll have access to reports, such as how many subscribers you have, optional notifications when a new subscriber signs up, etc.

12. You can create a *campaign* (auto sequence of special-purpose email events), This enables you to evolve your campaign(s) as you collect subscribers and their interests change,

13. Integrates with commerce platforms (e.g., Shopify, WooCommerce…). This may not be important to

you now, but if you plan to sell your books directly from your website, for example (without some other online retailer in between you and your buyers), these *integrations* will become important to you. Don't worry about that now.

The bad news:

1. Some work is required to integrate MC with FB, Twitter, to share in a campaign or for *QR codes* (phone camera scans... think 'bar code scanner' – which is a quick 'n easy way to send anyone with a smart phone to your signup form),
2. MC has good articles explaining the process for each, but they can be confusing (you don't get what you don't pay for!),
3. You want easier yet? It'll cost you from $10/month (for growing businesses) to $200/month (for pro marketers),
4. Plus whatever you're paying for a hosting service,
5. Plus a custom domain name (that is, your own web address like **GKJurrens.com**),
6. Plus premium site templates (this all adds up in a hurry, which is why I advocate as many free or entry level plans at first until you decide what you need or want *and are willing to pay for*).

Bottom line: pick your tools based on your objectives and your budget. Choose from lots of free stuff if you have the time and technical acumen. Easier EMA solutions cost more but give you value if you can afford (justify) it.

15

SUSTAIN YOUR MARKETING

THE LEARNING LOOP

There is no shortage of free information out there once you get yourself *in the learning loop.* Leverage others' (my?) experience to accelerate your learning  curve. By subscribing to email lists of some of the resources described already, you'll get regular emails to view, to learn, and to optionally buy additional education or tools.

OTHER BOOK MARKETING THOUGHTS:

Dave Chesson (**Kindlepreneur.com**) earns six figures by writing and helping other writers. His strategy is to write books, get a good editor, have a good marketing plan. Then select the right:

1. Book Cover: Derek Murphy's **DIYBookCovers** (with which I have some experience) or hire a professional cover designer,

2. Book's **title** and **sub-title** are important. Dave's research is invaluable,

3. **Good book description formatting**: Dave's free *description generator* formats great-looking book descriptions on your digital store front sales pages (avoids programming complexities). *I use it for every book I publish and sell*, although now some platforms are integrating programming-free formatting.

4. Did I mention that it's free, at least at the time of this writing?

5. **Networking: Partner with other authors** within your genre to increase your website traffic, add highly targeted leads (people who really like you or your work) to your email list, boost your book sales (ads, personal or media appearances, reader magnets…), seek reviews and endorsements, seek introductions to editors, agents, self-publishers or traditional publishers. But all of this takes time. Even if you publish traditionally, you'll still need to invest in these activities ("ain't nothin' for nothin' "). Writing conferences are a great way to kick-start such networking. Facebook groups can also be effective (with sustained effort).

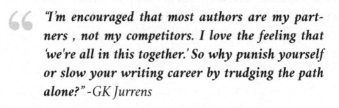

"I'm encouraged that most authors are my part-ners , not my competitors. I love the feeling that 'we're all in this together.' So why punish yourself or slow your writing career by trudging the path alone?" -GK Jurrens

Part of establishing your writers' <u>partner network</u> should include **social networking sites** *for writers* such as:

1. **Writer's Cafe** ("An Online Writing Community"),
2. **Writing Room** ("Everything Writing"),
3. **AuthorMedia.Social** (a social media platform exclusively for authors),
4. **NaNoWriMo** (**Na**tional **No**vel **Wri**ting **Mo**nth). Every November, but good stuff can be yours all year 'round). You should seriously consider participating in at least one *NaNoWriMo* no matter where you find yourself on your literary journey. It's thrilling and a great way to meet other writers. Plus, at the end of November (even if you just started on Halloween), stick with it and you'll have a first draft of your very own novel! I highly recommend this exhilarating experience. But like the rest of this stuff, ya gotta wanna.

Join a variety of **Facebook groups** for authors. There are many. Search for groups with *author* or *kindle* or *writers* or *book* in their name). Examples:

1. *Authors* on the Road,
2. *Readers* and *Authors,*
3. Creative Fiction *Writing,*
4. *Writers* and *Readers* Unite,
5. Indie *Authors* Book Promotion Page...

You benefit from helping writers, endorsing the work of other successful writers *and* by being an ambassador for their work. So they'll be an ambassador for *yours.*

A specific example (and there are *many* others)... Dave

Chesson (Kindlepreneur) helps other writers by offering freebies on how to optimize your *visibility* (an author's biggest challenge beyond writing the book is getting your book discovered by potential buyers of your book). And here I am sharing his name and his work with you! Check out Dave's free article on selecting the right keyword strategy for selling your fiction on the most popular digital store front. He offers another article for non-fiction authors) at https://kindlepreneur.com/kindle-keywords-fiction-author-strategy/

1. A great article (one of many) that suggests strategies so your book becomes visible to more readers (potential buyers)
2. By using a *process to use keywords that people were already using to search for books, but weren't too competitive.*
3. Getting your book in front of more eyes,
4. Understanding fiction buyers' mentality,
5. Strategies to employ, e.g., niche vs broad, similar book ('also bought') mentions, and what <u>not</u> to do. One effective example: **niche down** to a very specific *ideal reader* and then target that reader with specific search keywords, book covers, book titles, book blurbs (back covers of print books) and book descriptions on your books' sales pages.

SEARCH KEYWORD ANALYSIS

Approximately 5,000 new books are published *daily.* Readers find new books to read on major digital store fronts by searching for them. It is critically important to know what *keywords* they use in their searches so you can identify your book with the most popular *keywords*. That geometrically increases the odds of your book's *discoverability*.

Using analysis tools like **Publisher Rocket** (PR offers a free trial, then a $97 one-time charge) you associate optimal search *keywords* with your book for sale. This is a complex topic you dare *not* relegate to guesswork:

1. General search terms (how readers find your book) are not good enough to ensure your book's "*findability*."
2. *PR* drills down to keyword *synonym* analysis. This is where the good stuff is buried.
3. So within "Fantasy," for example, you look for not just "Wizard", but "a man who uses magic" and you get more usable stuff to decide what to write about based on your marketing plan.
4. **BUT if the book's no good,** your rankings will sink downward no matter what (guiding principle: your book's gotta be good!).

The crux of this illustrative article on educating yourself (for free) on marketing your book using optimal keywords:

1. **Broad terms** (search keywords) **are useless**,
2. **Niche terms** exist, **are better**, and will deliver more buyers to your book. This stresses the importance of *niching down*,
3. BUT what if you don't want to sell books just to Kindle device owners? No problem. Your readers can read your Kindle edition on any smart device:

4. ***Pro Tip:*** *Reader apps are available free for any smart device (all smartphones, tablets and computers) right from the most popular digital store front's sales page.* <u>I always remind potential buyers of my books of this because so many are unaware, and this can negatively affect your sales.</u>

BOOK REVIEWS

You need to solicit reviews for your book:

1. But don't wait until it's published!
2. Once you are almost ready for publication (final draft), solicit *beta readers* (sources include writers groups, critique circles, bloggers, social media friends/followers, professional reviewers, other authors with name recognition who are willing to read your manuscript and offer a review in return for you plugging their stuff with *your* followers on social media, your blog(s), etc. Ask and keep asking!
3. Solicit your **author network** mentioned earlier (you *are* developing and nurturing this important part of your marketing eco-system, aren't you? If not, get off your ass and get to work),
4. Cite those reviews (quotes and sources) in your campaign on your own web site, in social media posts, in email blasts to your subscribers, etc).
5. You can pay someone to write reviews, but be cautious here and know some digital store front's

rules: you can't pay someone for ratings (e.g., 5-star reviews).

6. Also, be aware that even *verified purchasers* can't post reviews unless they spend at least $50 per year on their web site (yeah, I know),

7. You *can* post reviews you've received directly (from within emails, verbally, etc.) as *editorial reviews* (you include them manually on your book's sales page). *Do not ignore this important opportunity!*

8. Solicit professional reviews on sites such as *BookBub*, the world's largest book promotion site. This can be costly, **but** you can gain visibility for your book and connect with readers on this popular site for free. To learn how, read **BookBub Reviews: Great For Readers & Authors** by Dave Chesson (yeah, he offers a lot of great resources to authors),

In parting, I sincerely hope you've found this brief compilation useful to your growth as a writer, publisher and marketer. It is but a brief survey, but offers access to a wealth of experience from across this industry. Please patronize the deeper resources available from the list of brilliant authors in **Appendix B.**

Write on, my friends!

APPENDIX A: CAPSTONE CASE STUDY: BLACK BLIZZARD

A NOVEL BY GK JURRENS

∼

I've recently published an ambitious project. ***Black Blizzard*** is a historical crime novel (fiction). It's getting very good early returns.

I employed the process you've read about in this book. You should choose whatever process works for you, but do choose and use a process. That's how you improve as a writer over time and across multiple writing projects.

I started this particular project with a general idea for a book and with the choice of a genre I wanted to try for the first time. After researching the historical period that I would flesh out with fictional characters in 1930s America, I became excited and solidified my desire to commit to this project.

From there, using the author tools described in this book, I envisioned a small cast of characters with specific and dramatic relationships to one another. So I drew a diagram, something I call a *relationship map*, which is a visual representation of who the characters are and how I foresee them interacting within the story. I *interviewed* each character to better understand each of them, starting with a photo for each I downloaded from the Internet. I used that photo as the genesis for creating that character's personality.

Next, I brainstormed a series of *what-if questions* about the story to get my creative juices flowing. I keep the answers to those questions around as a reference to keep me on track with my early thinking for this book.

From there, I created a list of *big moments*, each with an expected outcome and at least one surprise consequence. That gave me enough to generate a *scene list*. I could then flesh out each scene with its own setting, more character detail, the character's goal, obstacle and a reaction to the action for that scene. I'd add some new information, and of course, something unexpected. I'd repeat this process for every scene.

Let's take a look, but keep in mind, this is still raw, but nicely illustrates my process.

∽

Black Blizzard
(was *Jake's Flame*)
by GK Jurrens

Initial Book Idea: A young couple (Jake Hardt and Sophie Bairns) falls in love during the Great Depression in 1930s America against all odds. They come from very different backgrounds but discover their mutual strength in the face of adversity. By using that strength to defend their family and their community, they draw local adversaries together to form an unbreakable bond. That bond enables them to defend their community from a common enemy—big city mobsters intent on corrupting their rural Northwest Iowa community with booze and drugs. The main characters are based on the true life experiences of the author's parents, but diverge from true life for dramatic effect (higher physical and emotional stakes, complicating factors, etc).

Genre: Historical Fiction
Sub-genre: Gritty Romantic Crime Drama

Relationship Map:

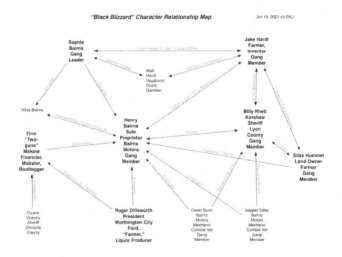

" What-if " Questions:

- *What if* Jake and Sophie meet, fall in love and marry much to the angst of Sophie's parents, especially her father, Henry Bairns?

- *What if* Henry sets out to buy at-risk Chevy dealerships across the midwest and gets in trouble with his financiers, his *bankers*?

- *What if* an affluent but aging farmer named Silas Hummel rents a farm to Jake who very soon can't pay the rent? What will Silas do? What will Jake do?

- *What if* Henry's *bankers* are also involved in bootlegging and smuggling, among other nefarious vices?

- *What if* Henry gets on the wrong side of these bankers and needs some rough 'n tumble help? What if that's Jake, his drunken cousin Walt, and/or some old friends who would do anything for Jake or for Henry? Or *especially* for little Sophie?

- *What if* Jake then needs to choose (internal conflict) between danger (external conflict), his love for Sophie (emotional conflict), breaking the law (ethical conflict), and loyalty to Sophie's father (familial conflict), even though Henry doesn't like Jake very much, except for his love of Sophie, his only daughter who is also handicapped? Maybe the crew that saves their rural community from Chicago ruffians is Jake, Jake's cousin Walt, his landlord and Henry's customer Silas, along with the local sheriff (Billy Rhett Kershaw) who carries his own emotional baggage?

- *What if* Sophie ends up being the unifying strength of this *gang* of erstwhile adversaries to save her father, his business, his family and their community? What will each character have to give up to achieve success in this quest?

- *What if* Henry is a misogynist early on, but otherwise a likable fellow, if not somewhat snooty? Maybe he changes because of his daughter Sophie as she comes of age, demonstrates her strength, admonishes her father, and *that* changes his attitude toward women in general?
- *What if* there's a complication: Sophie gets pregnant at the worst possible time and this causes other complications (her baseline physical condition, the fight with the bankers, etc)? Now the clock is ticking for reasons other than their father's business dilemma.
- *What if* Jake and cousin Walt start on rough ground with the Lyon County Sheriff Billy Kershaw, but later partner with him and Silas as all grow to trust each other; however, not before several adversarial confrontations?
- *What if* Sheriff Billy tries to evict Jake & Sophie (per her father Henry who is ruthless enough— early on—to evict his own daughter, secretly hoping she'll leave that pitiable dirt farmer and return home to him and her mother, Hilda)?
- But later, as Jake proves his undying love for Henry's daughter, Sophie, and by extension for her family, *what if* Henry realizes Jake is a strong and honorable man, and that he needs Jake's deadly serious help with these scary bankers?
- *What if* all is then forgiven, and Henry calls off the sheriff, vouches for Jake and his itinerant cousin?
- Then *what if* the *gang* (Jake, Sophie, Walt, Silas, Henry and Sheriff Billy) all partner within the community to defend against the ruthless bootleggers from a big city out east—Chicago?

- *What if* the *out-east money guys* the gang is fighting are just a front for another *local* businessman (a surprise twist later in the story) who harbors a vendetta for Henry Bairns?
- *What if* a competing auto dealer, *the Ford guy*—owner of a Ford dealership from a neighboring town—who's been burned by some of Bairns Chevrolet Motors less scrupulous business dealings? Maybe he wasn't screwed by Henry himself, but by one of his employees?
- *What if* the Ford guy, Roger Dillworth, runs booze from his nearby farm into Nebraska using his dealership's panel vans?
- *What if* Roger conspires with the bankers against Henry (unbeknownst to Henry until near the end of the story) so Dillworth can steal Henry's dealership? Why? To buy local respectability?
- *What if* one of Sheriff Billy's deputies is found murdered in a ditch?
- *What if* suspicion is initially cast upon Billy for this heinous crime? Motive associated with his personal baggage? Who frames him? A rival sheriff from a neighboring county who we find later is in league with Dillworth, and maybe the Chicago bootleggers?
- *What if* Henry finds out about the bootlegging operation out on Dillworth's nearby farm, and the gang sneaks out there after someone spots several suspicious trucks transiting out that way where they discover the connection between Roger and Henry's *bankers* (the Chicago bootleggers)?
- Then *what if* Roger's *better angel* ultimately compels him to team up with Sophie's *gang* to bring down

the Chicago mob because he regrets getting tangled up with them against his neighbors? Or is this too far-fetched? Dunno.

Premise:

From these *what-if questions*, it's time to create a tighter *premise* for the book's entire story. I came up with a couple of paragraphs and then revised them at least a dozen times until it reflected precisely the story I wanted to write. It will, no doubt, be revised a few dozen more times, and that's okay. This is my DRAFT PREMISE:

 1932 Iowa isn't as grim as other parts of America. Yet. Still, times are getting tougher as crops wither in the fields. Money and food are scarce, but that's the least of it.

A penniless farmer, Jake Hardt falls for an affluent but crippled girl from town named Sophie. But her influential father, Henry Bairns, throws every conceivable obstacle in their way; that is, until he needs Jake's unique brand of help, along with a few other locals, to fight off big city ruffians from out east who try to steal his business, ruin his family and corrupt their community.

Then Henry learns that not only is Jake honorable and courageous, although socially awkward, he truly is deeply in love with his daughter, and not just stalking her dowry. So under the surprise leadership of Henry's little Sophie, they all partner to defeat the band of Chicago bootleggers bent on destroying their rural community.

But success is a long shot. At best.

Ed: See the updated premise after reader feedback and maybe two dozen revisions (it's is important to get this right):

The summer of 1933 feels like Armageddon. Crops are dead, jobs are gone, and hope is dying. Even breathing grows difficult in zero-visibility dust storms called black blizzards. Worse, Lyon County Sheriff Billy Rhett Kershaw finds his young deputy murdered. About the same time, his friends and neighbors begin killing themselves.

In the midst of all this, when Sheriff Billy, with a few deputized locals, learns that an organized group of career criminals from Chicago threaten a local businessman and his family in the small town of George, Iowa, they look for a connection between these brutal newcomers and the mysterious deaths. Or is something far more sinister going on?

If you love historical crime fiction, or would like to explore it, get lost in "Black Blizzard."

BIG MOMENTS:

Armed with this draft *premise* for the project and lots of questions to answer, with more questions brimming over the confines of my notebook of ideas, I could already conceive more than two dozen *big moments* that would keep the tale engaging. So I mapped my initial answers to my *what-if questions* into the following *big moments*:

1. Jake and Sophie fall in love and marry. They decide to move to Jake's rented farm.

Expected outcome: the inevitability of this couple's decision based on their flirtatious liaison that spanned several months.

Unexpected outcome: Vociferous objections from Sophie's parents, Henry & Hilda Bairns.

2. Jake takes in his drunken older cousin, Walt.

Expected: He vowed he had quit drinking and would earn his keep—as promised.

Unexpected: He would not honor his commitment to earn his keep—as promised—and that Jake seemed not to mind but allowed him to stay anyway. At least this was Sophie's point of view. They also doubted whether he had indeed put the plug in the jug. Plus, they learn Walt is a talented gambler.

3. Jake attempts to sell his revolutionary automated hay-baling invention.

Expected: This is a fine invention.

Unexpected: Someone else has produced one almost as good, but for far less money.

4. Jake is in arrears on the farm's rent.

Expected: Pressure from his landlord, Silas, to pay or vacate.

Unexpected: After always giving Jake extra time to pay, Silas suddenly says he and Sophie must leave the farm immediately. Peculiar.

5. Henry conspires with Jake's landlord, Silas, to evict Jake and Sophie.

Expected: Henry sends Sheriff Billy to serve the papers.

Unexpected: Billy's heart really isn't in it, and neither is Silas's.

6. Henry commits to buying four failing Chevy dealerships in Iowa and Nebraska.

Expected: The price is low because the dealerships are failing, but that's why Henry chose them. He knows he can turn them around for a huge profit.

Unexpected: The ease with which he was able to get all the money he needed, and more.

7. Henry discovers his venture capitalist, his banker, is a mobbed-up bootlegger and loan shark who quickly graduates to intimidation and physical threats.

Expected: There would be complications as a result of who supplied the money.

Unexpected: Unreasonable demands would mean that it was likely Henry would lose Bairns Motors by defaulting on impossible terms, or from fear of violence.

8. Henry reluctantly asks Jake and Walt for their help, but isn't exactly sure what he's asking for.

Expected: Jake would say no because of their mutual adversarial history.

Unexpected: Jake not only agreed, but enthusiastically offered any and all help, as if he was trying to prove the family bond that had always been there despite Henry's bad behavior earlier.

9. Initial confrontation with the banker on the phone.

Expected: Fireworks.

Unexpected: Understated and implied threats of violence to Henry *and to his extended family.*

10. Henry is accused of being a Communist.

Expected: This is part of a threat made by his banker, Finn Malone, to destroy his reputation if Henry didn't relinquish ownership of Bairns Motors.

Unexpected: They have details of Henry's past that only a close friend could know.

11. The gang (Jake, Walt, Silas, Henry, Billy) realize they need to work together somehow, but struggle with their adversarial history.

Expected: Their mutual commitment to the community.

Unexpected: How hard it would be to find common ground, and frightening implications for the town if taken over by these gangsters as a distribution point for illegal booze. George City, Iowa, is strategically located far away from Chicago where the G-men are all over the mob, but close to a major source of booze production—Roger Dillworth's farm—*and* to a major source of alcohol consumption —Omaha, Nebraska. Bairns Motors would lend a credible cover to the mob's presence in Lyon County. At least that's the assumption.

12. Sophie pulls the gang together.

Expected: Sophie's charm would have a soothing effect, and her firm common sense could not be ignored.

Unexpected: That she'd become the driving force to unify them against a common enemy.

13. Omaha police arrest Silas while he's in that city shopping for farm implements.

Expected: Corrupt police and local politicians.
Unexpected: *No apparent reason for* Silas to be arrested. Henry's banker is involved. Now even Sheriff Billy has to watch his back as the tendrils of corruption already reach deeper into the region than earlier suspected. The Great Depression has everyone desperate to feed their families, or from naked greed.

14. Sophie personally recruits *muscle—t*wo of Henry's mechanics from the dealership with combat experience from the Great War.

Expected: This is a big ask.
Unexpected: How readily the mechanics, Owen and Seppel, agree to help despite Sophie's warnings of potential danger.

15. Sophie seeks information from her childhood friend Edith Erdlinger even though she is from one of the few Catholic families in town who still lives in the old neighborhood just down the street from Henry and Hilda's house. Edith always was a bit of a *bad girl*.

Expected: She knows where all the *whoopee parties* are.
Unexpected: She knows that *the Ford guy* from Worthington City, Roger Dillworth, supplies booze to a few select locals as a favor—often traded for info about Henry and Bairns Motors.

16. The gang (via Sheriff Billy) finds out *the Ford guy* from Worthington City (Roger Dillworth) is into bootlegging as

a major side hustle, just like Henry's *banker* from Chicago. Coincidence? Or is Roger's Ford dealership in Worthington City just his side business?

Expected: The enemy is from Chicago.

Unexpected: The real enemy may very well be another area businessman who also owns a farm between George and Worthington City.

17. Silas sells as much corn as he can grow directly to Roger at a significantly higher price than Silas can get at the local grain elevator in George City, and that's how Silas can afford property, a new car, etc.

Expected: Silas is a friend to Henry and a silent supplier to Roger.

Unexpected: Silas doesn't know that Roger is trying to ruin Henry in conjunction with efforts of the Chicago mob, nor does he know what his corn is used for, although he suspects. He volunteers to set up Roger. This would have a ripple-effect as it disrupts the flow of booze from Roger's farm to Omaha, and the flow of cash from Omaha to Chicago.

18. The *gang* plans and executes a covert mission to learn more of the operation at Dillworth's farm between George and Worthington City. They spot the banker's distinctive automobile, a unique red and black 1929 Duesenberg Roadster with its beige canvas top *and* a truck larger in volume than most farm trucks.

Expected: Roger Dillworth (the Ford guy from Worthington City) is distilling hooch on his farm.

Unexpected: Roger is tangled up with Henry's banker,

Finn Malone. Also, the volume of booze coming out of Roger's farm is huge and is being shipped out by the truckload.

19. Discourage Finn Malone's Chicago backers by deflecting their focus. They're all about bootlegging, not car dealerships - that's Malone's gig on behalf of Roger Dillworth. Our Lyon County gang destroys the industrial-strength still on Roger's farm. That disrupts product distribution to the Omaha mob. This puts the heat on Malone until his Chicago backers lose interest in Bairns Motors. But Malone is now obsessed (now a private vendetta) and he won't give up.

Expected: That they'd destroy Roger's huge still (or at least attempt to do so).

Unexpected: The Chicago mob loses interest in Henry's dealership, but Malone does not.

20. Confrontation with Malone and his gunsels at Chautauqua outside Worthington City.

Expected: A confrontation was inevitable, and the Lyon County gang involves G-men from Chicago for an unsuccessful "sting" attempt.

Unexpected: Members of Chautauqua come to their aid when things get rough.

21. The Lyon County gang celebrates saving Henry's dealership and having kept gangsters from invading their peaceful but dusty little corner of NW Iowa. At least for the time being.

Expected: Happy ending.

Unexpected: Sophie's water breaks during the celebration at Bairns Motors. Sheriff Billy drives her and Jake at breakneck speed to the hospital in nearby Sibley over on Route 60 via Iowa State Road 9.

STORY STRUCTURE:

Now it's time to lay these *big moments* into a framework that will resonate with readers. Remember the three act structure from **Chapter 6**?

I won't punish you with my entire layout, but for illustrative purposes, I laid the initial big moments into **Act One**'s *ordinary world* of the farm, the town and a few of the main characters (Jake, Sophie, Henry), a *hook* intended to quickly engage readers (a gangster and his driver scream toward the small town of George, Iowa. En route, they dump the body of a young Lyon County Sheriff's deputy into a country ditch).

Next, the *inciting incident* draws our hero Jake into the story. He falls hard for the rich girl in town—Henry's daughter. Henry will eventually need Jake's help fighting off murderous gangsters bent on taking his business in Act One's *climax*. Jake was depending on his big get-rich-quick scheme to save him and Sophie from homelessness, but the invention fails, creating a grim picture of their future (*first plot turning point*).

Act Two, the longest act, will see a lot of action. Lines between enemies and allies are drawn, then blurred. Relationships grow increasingly complicated by the story's *midpoint*, aka its *mirror moment*. Stakes get raised, more *obstacles* surface, we see ultimatums delivered, and the forces of evil in the story seem to be in control as the bad guys close in (*rising action*). This results in a variety of ethical conflicts and a violent *confrontation* resulting in shocking revelations and a casualty. The second act concludes with a *second plot turning* *point* (often called the "dark night of the soul"). The good guys' plan has failed (*try/fail cycles*). They have lost a battle with serious consequences. Jake's cousin Walt is severely injured and there is plenty of guilt over that. Jake and the gang discover a shocking *revelation:* their enemy isn't their *only* enemy, and a neighbor is really the primary antagonist. All seems hopeless and it seems the situation can't get any worse.

Act Three begins with our gang of good guys, the *Lyon County gang,* on the verge of giving up. Unexpectedly, crippled Sophie rallies the gang, admonishes them for feeling sorry for themselves, and emerges as the de facto leader who gives them courage and direction. Against overwhelming odds, they go into hiding to recover from their earlier defeat and to plan their final battle in relative safety, or at least in secrecy. They will suffer one more defeat but ultimately snatch an unexpected victory before vanquishing their enemies, at least for the foreseeable future (*climax*). They achieve this with a surprise ally from the enemy camp, and an appearance of federal ATF officers (*G-men*) who save the day. Every one of the gang has undergone changes (internal and external), some for the worse, but most for the better. The future is bright after the long darkness (*resolution*). Hardships remain (Great Depression, Dust Bowl…), but they've rescued their humanity and their community—for now.

SCENE LIST:

These scene titles are just placeholders, but they enable me to start fleshing out each one in pursuit of a rough-hewn first draft. I'll decide on more appropriate titles and sequence later, but these become the crucibles for firing the heat of the *big moments* listed above within our draft 24-chapter story structure.

Act I (hero & ordinary world):

- Prey and predator - body dump
- A really bad day - 1932 'ordinary' world
- The farm - a ten-dollar smile and hog shit
- Sophie & Hilda - strong women, cashmere eyes
- From afar - the spark ignited between Jake and Sophie
- Sophie's father - frigid beginnings with Jake
- Emerging love - first molten touch
- Goes like sixty - fifty horses, the smell of calf-skin
- Married and on the farm - endless love, endless toil
- Taking in cousin Walt - bathtub gin in the morning, money in the belt
- In the Kitchen - mile-high loaves, butter 'n jam
- A peculiar traveling salesman - Fuller Brush. Watkins or confidence man?
- Grasping at straws - on the lamb
- Call to adventure - gambling past and present intrigue
- Head in the sand - smoldering conflict, a drunk in the house
- Pull out the rug - no loans for genius inventors and dreamers

(16 chapters)

Act II (exploring new world & bad guys close in):

- Enemies and allies - frustration builds, tensions escalate, past sins catch up, rent's due or homeless,

- Games and trials - Jake pitches his invention to the S&L but gets shot down, cousin Walt offers all of his ill-gotten gains still stashed in his "girdle"
- Earning respect - Jake exhibits a working model of his steam-powered auto-baler invention at the Lyon County tractor meet, raises over twenty dollars
- Forces of evil - Jake & Sophie receive an eviction notice from the farm, so they arm themselves to stay; Henry's banker, Finn Malone, threatens Sophie's father, Henry. Malone plans to take Henry's Chevy dealership with threats of destroying Henry's reputation, or worse rain heinous violence on him and his entire extended family (even the family dog, which they don't have)
- Problem revealed - Sophie discovers her father is behind the eviction notice; Henry discovers the banker funding his purchase of several troubled Chevy dealerships is really a bootlegger and a mobster; Henry's competition, Roger *the Ford guy* from a nearby town, is in league with the crooked banker; Roger is intent on taking over Henry's Chevy dealership at any cost
- Truth and ultimatum - Malone commands Henry to sell and retire or he'd get him labeled a Communist with the G-men; Sophie finally finds out that Jake's cousin Walt has been feeding Jake his gambling winnings so as not to lose the farm; Sophie discovers her father's tribulations with his banker through her mother Hilda
- Victim to warrior - Sophie convinces Sheriff Billy and Henry to ask for Jake's help in dealing with Malone, Dillworth; Sophie also charms two of Henry's rough 'n tumble mechanics to bring their

combat experience from the Great War to bear. They form a united front & vow to push back against the hooligan invaders, hard

- Plan of attack - During a covert reconnaissance by *Sophie's gang* to the Dillworth farm—discovering it's a major alcohol manufacturing/distribution depot—they see Henry's banker's car there. The plan: put Dillworth out of business, and the banker will lose interest in Henry's dealership
- Crucial role - Sophie charges Jake and Walt to spy on Dillworth at his dealership by pretending to be car shoppers, and if possible through the use of Walt's boyish charm, gain the confidence of one of Dillworth's (female) employees
- Direct conflict - battle at the Dillworth farm, objective: blow up the still.
- Surprise failure - Sheriff Billy coordinated the Dillworth farm attack with neighboring county Sheriff Duane Graves. The attack fails. Walt is wounded. Henry's banker, Finn "Two-guns" Malone retaliates by burning down Jake's barn, including their entire savings (including the bulk of Walt's contributions to Jake's stash) under the barn's floor planks. The fire also destroys their meager harvest of hay in the haymow, and the fire also kills their horse, Queenie
- Shocking revelation - The attack on the Dillworth farm was thwarted because Sheriff Duane Graves, Sheriff Billy's *friend*, is on Dillworth's payroll and betrayed them.

(12 chapters)

Act III (defeat & victory):

- <u>Giving up</u> - Walt is in tough shape, Jake is torn with guilt over it, Sheriff Billy feels helpless and depressed over Sheriff Graves' betrayal, and all suffer from crippling emotions. They consider acceding to Malone's demands to avoid further bloodshed
- <u>Pep talk</u> - Only Sophie refuses to be inconsolable or to accept defeat. She shames the men into getting over themselves and to realize there is no future in succumbing to bullies. The men realize she is absolutely right.
- <u>Seizing the sword</u> - The gang goes to ground at one of Silas's lesser properties. Sophie assigns Henry's two mechanics with combat experience to guard their perimeter. Sheriff Billy calls the feds in from Chicago, not knowing who they can trust locally, not even his own deputies. Henry sets up a meeting with Malone at the Dillworth farm with a ruse: to turn over his dealership.
- <u>Ultimate defeat</u> - Before Henry arrives, the gang, less Walt (old Silas, Jake, Billy and Henry's two combat vet mechanics—Owen and Seppel) arrive early, armed. A skirmish ends up with the gang getting captured, disarmed and badly beaten. Seppel is killed during the skirmish. Henry rushes in to appeal for mercy. The gang now realizes they *never* had *any* chance of defeating these experienced and heavily armed criminals—a fool's errand fueled by irrational passion
- <u>Unexpected victory</u> - The gang of five, including Henry, are about to be executed when the feds swoop in and save the day.
- <u>Bittersweet return</u> - The gang returns to normal life… changed. Their safety is likely short-lived

and bittersweet. Jake's challenges, the same as before, now seem trivial. The gang has grown closer, now friends, and more confident, having shared the field of battle together.

- Rebirth - Each gang member has graduated from ambition to service, essentially witnessing the death of their former selves, and one of their own. They acknowledge their renewed commitment to their families, to each other, and to their community.

(7 chapters)

Credit for this framework goes to Derek Murphy and his amazing 24-chapter-novel *Scrivener* template that I used as a general story structure framework.

WHAT'S NEXT?

While I am still researching the 1930s and interviewing the few folks still living who lived through that period, or who have vivid memories from others who have, I clearly now have written enough to start fleshing out what is likely to result in thirty-five or more chapters which I will ultimately separate, combine and shuffle further. I've learned this sort of flexibility is necessary to stomp out plot holes and other discontinuities in the story line as it evolves. It's all part of the writing and editing process (*after* the first draft is completed). But I already possess more than sufficient bones for an 80,000- to 100,000-word novel, maybe even a 120,000-word epic.

A word of caution. If you choose to price your book competitively, I suggest you establish a target of no more than about 70,000 words for your own book. Remember, printing on demand (POD), and commensurate pricing of the product (your book) is based on printing costs, which is higher with more pages. Many best sellers in this genre weigh in at about 70,000 words, unless it grows to epic proportions. Then high printing costs will impact profitability if priced competitively.

Just for reference, Kindle Direct Publishing (KDP), prints author copies about as affordably as any POD vendor. Author copies enable you to buy copies of your books in order to sell them yourself. This way, you make more money per book because you sell them directly to your readers and avoid paying a portion of your profit to another vendor for order processing, shipping and handling on a per unit basis (a.k.a. *fulfillment*).

Below you can see some recent examples from my own *backlist* illustrating page- and word-counts (in thousands of words, or k words) followed by KDP ***printing cost for author copies*** that I order for selling directly to customers:

- *This book*: 166 pages = 28k words = $2.84
- *Underground*: 236 pages = 48k words = $3.68
- *Dangerous Dreams*: 374 pages = 95k words = $5.34
- *Fractured Dreams*: 378 pages = 96k words = $5.39
- *Mean Streets*: 454 pages = 105k words = $6.30
- *Post Earth*: 512 pages = 128k words = $6.99

So the difference between the cost above (plus shipping costs), and my asking price per copy will comprise my profit per copy. Don't forget to add or include tax. I usually order a print run large enough to outlast four to six weeks of direct sales. It takes about that long to receive another shipment of author copies from most any print-on-demand vendor. The more copies I order (generally speaking), the cheaper the shipping cost.

Any retail pricing model (similar to most distributors and fulfillment channels) **paints a less rosy picture**. I'll offer one example to illustrate. As you can see above, **this book's paperback edition will cost me $2.84 to bind and print.** I typically choose the royalty model that yields the most profit for me with them managing the complexities and the costs of fulfillment (managing the customer relationship, orders, shipping, handling, tax collection, reporting…). That's called the 60% royalty model for print books, which means **if I specify my asking price for this book on KDP to be $7.99** (which is already rather costly for a short book like this one), **my royalty (profit) will be only $1.95**. They calculate and offer these numbers to me before I hit the publish button.

With their 40% royalty model, the profitability profile worsens. **I would make only *thirty-five cents* per copy**. At **$6.99 retail, I would make NOTHING**; however, the 40% model would enroll my title for *expanded distribution* to more *sales channels beyond one channel.* Roll the dice, my friend. But eccentricities of these royalty and channels topics are beyond the scope of this book and differ by vendor. **For now, just remember this:**

> **Word-counts and subsequent page-counts matter!**

So you can see if I charge a retail price of $8 to $15 for a book (signed by the author!), I make a decent profit *by selling these books myself*. But a $3 difference in *printing cost* per book can mean the difference between reasonable profit and no profit at all *if you're selling your books online through a retailer!* So keep all of this in mind as you pen your own masterpiece.

> ***My lesson learned:*** if my story will exceed 60k to 70k words (programs like *Scrivener*, *Microsoft Word* and *Vellum* incorporate a word-count feature), I will seriously consider splitting up the story into a series of individual but related books. Otherwise, I could price myself out of competition.

APPENDIX B: RESOURCES

Leverage this list of useful resources which are either free (where indicated), or average $3 each as ebooks or pre-owned paperbacks from used book stores (some of my favorite haunts).

Below are my favorites from the many dozens (hundreds?) I've devoured over the last five years:

WRITING RESOURCES (ALPHABETICAL ORDER BY AUTHOR):

1. Ackerman and Puglisi: **Writers Helping Writers Series**,
2. Charles Baxter: **The Art of Subtext**,
3. James Scott Bell: **Write Your Novel from the Middle**,
4. Mark Dawson's free ebook, **Writing a Page-Turner**,
5. Chris Fox: **Write Fast, Write Smarter Series**,
6. Jane Friedman, free post: **How to Start Blogging**
7. Jane Friedman Blog: **General writing advice**,
8. Noah Lukeman: **The First Five Pages: A Writer's Guide to Staying Out of the Rejection Pile**,
9. NANOWRIMO (free): **National Novel Writing Month**,
10. Derek Murphy's **free Scrivener template** for a novel,
11. Joanna Penn: **Books for Writers**,
12. Karen Wiesner: **First Draft in 30 Days**.
13. Writer's Digest Books, Elements of Fiction Writing: **Beginnings, Middles and Ends, Conflict, Action and Suspense; Characters and Viewpoint**;
14. James Scott Bell: **Plot & Structure**.

AUTHOR BRANDING, PUBLISHING AND MARKETING RESOURCES:

1. Derek Murphy: **Guerrilla Publishing**,

2. Derek Murphy free ebook: **Book Marketing is Dead**,
3. Nick Stephenson's free ebook, **Reader Magnets**,
4. Tammy Labrecque's book, **Newsletter Ninja**,
5. David Wogahn: **My Publishing Imprint**,
6. David Wogahn: **The Book Review Companion,**
7. Ian Sutherland: **Advanced Twitter Strategies**,
8. **Author Media**: Innovative Book Promotion and *Novel Marketing* podcast (free).

SOLICITING TRADITIONAL PUBLISHERS:

1. **Writer's Market,** from Writer's Digest Books. This is a book where writers learn how to get published, market, and sell their writing (I prefer the print edition for highlighting publishers in my genre including small (easiest to get representation) to large (more difficult) publishers, detailed submission guidelines each require (follow them *rigorously)*, university presses, agents, editors, contests (some are free), etc. **"Writer's Market" is an invaluable resource whether you plan to traditionally publish or not.** But for a few bucks more, acquire the "Deluxe Edition" which also buys you online access to a host of useful resources like tracking submissions to publishers, query letters and agency contacts, all quickly and efficiently searchable.
2. Find a **Literary Agent** to represent you at https://www.janefriedman.com/find-literary-agent/
3. Another resource to find a **Literary Agent:** https://www.queryletter.com/blog/categories/finding-a-literary-agent

4. **Here is a helpful article on constructing Query Letters** to Traditional Publishing Houses, Publishing Advice, Sample Query Letters: https:// www.queryletter.com/post/161-examples-of-successful-query-letters-from-famous-authors

OTHER BOOKS BY GK JURRENS

≈

Contemporary Fiction (Thrillers)

- Dangerous Dreams: Dream Runners: Book 1
- Fractured Dreams: Dream Runners: Book 2

Historical Fiction (Great Depression Era Crime)

- Black Blizzard: A Lyon County Adventure
- Murder in Purgatory: A Lyon County Mystery

Futuristic Fiction (Paranormal Mystery Thrillers)

- Underground, Mayhem: Book 1
- Mean Streets, Mayhem: Book 2
- Post Earth, Mayhem: Book 3
- A Glimpse of Mayhem: Companion Guide to the Mayhem Trilogy

Poetry, Short Stories & Essays:

- The Poetic Detective: Investigate Rhyme with Reason

Non-fiction

- Why Write? Why Publish? Passion? Profit? Both?
- Moving a Boat and Her Crew

- Restoring a Boat and Her Crew

ABOUT THE AUTHOR

~

GK JURRENS WRITES WITH UNDILUTED PASSION.

He also teaches a nearly paperless writing and publishing methodology and workflow on the road. Most of the time, he and his wife live and travel in a motorhome when they're not spending time at their condo in Southwest Florida. They find wandering their beloved North America a source of endless inspiration.

After studying Liberal Arts, GK earned a Bachelor of Science degree in Business and a Master of Science degree in Management of Technology from the University of Minnesota, USA. He is the proud father of two adult children and the equally proud grandfather of three teenage grand-children.

Six years of government service preceded a successful three-decade career in global high-technology. GK and his partner indulged in more than a few years of sailing America's waterways, the Florida Keys, and the Eastern Caribbean from the British Virgin Islands to near the coasts of Venezuela and Trinidad.

GK continues to pursue his life-long penchant for the creative arts that include writing (prose and poetry), painting (watercolor), and traveling (now mostly within North America).

He plays his guitar and a growing collection of Native American flutes, some of which he crafted while living in the Arizona desert.

Quiet evenings, adventurous motorcycle rides and over-landing in the Jeep alongside his copilot and soulmate of more than half a century fills the action gaps and keeps him young (at heart, at least). If you wish to offer the author feed-back, for which he'd be grateful, consider emailing **gjur rens@yahoo.com** or visit **GKJurrens.com**.

Also follow GK on:

 goodreads.com/gkjurrens

 twitter.com/gjurrens1

 facebook.com/genejurrens

 instagram.com/gjurrens

 linkedin.com/in/gkjurrens

Made in the USA
Monee, IL
06 May 2023

32793103R00095